Sunday Mourning

Rhachelle Nicol'

Copyright © 2011 Rhachelle Johnson

All rights reserved.

ISBN: 0578088827
ISBN-13: 978-0578088822

My Mourning has turned to joy…

I must first thank God; he is definitely the head of my life. I thank God that when I asked him to show me my heart, he did just that. He was real with me and I had to get real with him. I thank God for my Father, I know he is looking down from heaven, saying "Good job baby girl". Mom, thank you for showing me what hardwork, determination and faith will produce. My sisters and my brother, you all know how I feel about each one of you. I was fortunate to be blessed with a bonus set of parents, in the form of my oldest sister and my only brother. You both are "old" lol. God saw what I would need to stay the course and whether or not I recognized it then, I get it now. And Ciceli, yes I wrote your name, I love you and keep your head up, there is an angel looking down on you from above.

I could go on and on, but I will say I have met some very encouraging and uplifting individuals throughout this process. I must say thank you to a close friend of mine, we finished college together and we now share a last name. We have become family. You already know who you are. There were so many conversations that we have shared whether over the phone or through text, that have given me that extra push when I wanted to give up. A special thanks to my little Sis, printing off the first chapter of what has evolved into a book, when I was just writing it on my blackberry.

Now before I get all teary-eyed, this one is for you "Kimmy". I don't think it was by coincidence that I used your name. I remember when I first shared with you a few pages and we just laughed it off. Through your life you showed me the power of a smile and how to give of myself freely. Through your death you taught me love, unconditional love. Rest in love cousin.

CONTENTS

	Foreword	i
1	Sunday Morning	1
2	New Levels, New Devils	13
3	Easy Come, Easy Go	25
4	A House Divided Cannot Stand	35
5	The Real World	47
6	Motherhood	54
7	A Leopard Doesn't Change Its Spots	64
8	Sou Ties – Soul Cries	72
9	Is There Life After Death	80
10	New State, Same State of Mind	83
11	What Doesn't Kill You Will Make You Stronger	87
12	Finding My Way Back	92
13	An Open Letter of Forgiveness	104
14	My Seed Will Be Blessed	109
15	Here Am I, Send Me	112

FOREWORD

"Ms. Johnson, this is Ms. Cook in the office at Thomas Elementary School. We got a call from your neighbor that Jeremiah locked himself out of the house and is outside with no shoes on and no supervision. We have also called campus police they are on their way to your house." The panic hit me so hard. I moved a few papers around on my desk, not really knowing how to respond but I knew I had to get to my child. What was going on, we went over everything before I left the house. "Jeremiah, if I leave you at home until lunch time, you need to finish your cereal, watch TV or play your video game, do not touch the stove, make a sandwich if you get hungry and do not go outside." I know he heard every word that I said but it was his first time at home and had I thought it all through I would have never let him stay. I thought Lord just get me home. I was angry, scared, confused and upset. Why didn't he listen?

I arrived home to be met by the officers. I had never been in trouble before in my life other than a couple traffic violations and a few parking tickets. "Are you Ms. Johnson?" the officer asked. "Yes, I am." "We need to talk to you to find out what's going on, can we come in?" I should have said no. I knew my house was a mess; I had just left it. A few dishes in the sink, clothes in the living room, unmade beds, blankets everywhere, I had an explanation for all, but did they want to hear it. "Come on in." I didn't have anything to hide my main concern was my son and being with him. "Well ma'am we received a call from your son's school informing us that he was unsupervised outside of his home and with a neighbor. Can you explain to us what happened?" I had been on the other side of these types of situations, I didn't have a story to make up just the truth to give, that's usually all it took and a verbal warning was all that was needed. "Well officer, last night I didn't get much sleep because my two youngest children were up for most of the night with fevers. At about 4:30am, I emailed my supervisor and informed her that I would not be into work. However, being that it was a court day for me, I knew that I had a lot of things that I needed to get submitted. 6:00am came fast and the children were feeling better with no fevers, so I decided to get everyone up and dressed to go. I usually drop Elijah off at school and Jeremiah and the three little ones go to the babysitter together. I was already running a little late and Jeremiah decided to make him a bowl of cereal a few minutes before we were walking out the door. He asked me if he could stay at home. I had never let him stay at home before, so I spelled out the rules. I told him to stay put inside, watch television, play your video game and make a sandwich if you get hungry, but you cannot go outside. He was fully dressed when I left, he said that he would stay put until I came to pick him up for school in the afternoon and the rest of us proceeded to leave the house." I understand that it may have not been the best situation or judgment call but my intentions were never to harm or put my child in harms way. With no set age for a child to be left at home, I didn't leave my house with the intent to commit a crime. Had I known I was committing a crime, he would have never been left. "Well ma'am, the problem we have is that he was left here with no adult supervision and no way to contact you in case of an emergency. When he locked himself out of the house he went to a few of the neighbor's home to contact you and he didn't get an answer and a message could not be left. Don't you work for the Department of Family Services? If he were my son, I would have grabbed him by the back of his neck and dragged him down the stairs kicking and screaming." "Yes officer, I do work for the Department of Family Services and I did not leave my home this morning with the intentions of breaking the law. I realize that there is no specific age stated that a child can be left at home and I see a lot of 6-year-old children walk to and from school daily. At the time, I saw nothing wrong with it and I was rushing to get out the house to get to work. We recently had a time clock system implemented and it has been causing me a great deal of anxiety being that I am caring for my 5 children on my own. My mother just left to go back to California and she usually helps me but we had a death in my family and in the same week that marks a year of my father passing. I've been really emotional and stressed out and I realize that hindsight is always twenty-twenty." A few minutes later more officers arrived. I was not sure what was going on but I didn't think that this situation was going to end like all the others I had experienced. All that I kept hearing was "Ms. Johnson we hold you at a higher standard because of your job." Since when did they create a separate law for people in my position? Since when did the law changed based on your occupation. Being a single mother of five is hard enough; I don't need extra laws because I have a job to take care of them.

"Ms. Johnson, I think you should call your job and let them know what's going on before they find out another way." I thought to myself what am I supposed to tell them other than the police are at my house no one had read me my rights or told me if I was going to jail. I called my boss and she was already in the office with her Supervisor. They already knew, that let me know that things wouldn't stop here and I wasn't getting a warning. "Ms. Johnson, you're under arrest." What was going on, where were they going to take my children? I didn't want them taking Jeremiah down to the intake. "Can I call my sister so that she can get my son? I don't want him going down there; he shouldn't have to go through this." They took my son out of the house and he would get to experience his mother's job in a totally different way. They took him out of the house and sent him away before they escorted me outside, patted me down and place the cold metal cuffs around my wrist. I was then asked to get in the back seat of the police car. Innocent until proven guilty is not an amendment is an overused cliché. I was treated like a criminal and housed amongst prostitutes and thieves. I would spend the next twenty-four hours behind bars; I didn't eat the food or use the restroom and was forced to sleep on hard wooden slate benches. They took forever to even book me into jail, so getting bailed out took that much longer and because of all the budget cuts they didn't release inmates at certain times. I cried and cried; praying was the last thing on my mind. All I could do was speak of the hatred towards my job. I had worked so hard for all the families and children I served. At times, I had put my job before my children, working long hours and sometimes, even weekends. But I shared so many similarities with the families I served; I had just found an escape.

I had been praying for a change. I wanted to spend more time with my family and be able to visit my extended family more. I was tired of living paycheck to paycheck and I just wanted some time to grieve the death of my father around family and friends. My co-workers had brought me condolences but it wasn't enough. So my prayers started but I never imagined this was where they would lead me. In a blink of an eye, I was stripped of all my hardwork, education, prestige and esteem. I didn't realize God was making room for the purpose, plan and promise for my life. That very moment came together with the thirty-one years of my past to give me a testimony and ministry. Now I must reflect in order to understand how I should proceed.

We all have an important date or two that we save in our mind and celebrate it when it comes around, whether it be a birthday, anniversary or holiday. Well March 3, 2010 is mine and it just so happens that it's not my birthday, anniversary or a holiday, but the date that marks the push I needed into my destiny. I'm still not clear how I arrived at this place or point in my life but I've learned how to embrace it, heal from it and share my story to hopefully heal others.

1 SUNDAY MORNING ~ HOME LIFE

Everybody always has a story to tell. Kimmy just told me her daddy went to jail last night for hitting her mom. I don't thinks its her real daddy though, she told me before that her real daddy was dead. I don't ask any questions because I don't have nothing to tell. I just sit and listen. You see my mother always said, "what goes on in this house stays in this house." I never thought much of it, I just kept it all to myself.

You see my friends always came to me with their problems anyways, I don't know how, but I always knew exactly what to say to make them forget about their problems. I had mastered that art so well. So while they were freeing themselves of the misery of their reality, I was filling my closet up with skeletons.

Kimmy was one of my childhood friends, my bestfriend. She shared all her secrets with me and I did my best to give her advice. Kimmy would come over to play or we would spend hours outside riding our bikes. She always came and knocked on my door. "Who is it?" "Its me Kimmy." I opened the door and let her in. "Hey Kimmy, I'm so sorry to hear about your mom and dad. What you been up to?" "Nothing much, just been helping my mom out around the house more." "She's having a hard time with the whole situation with my daddy. I rode my bike over here as soon as my mama got of the phone and filled me on what was going on. She was going to drop the charges, but she doesn't have a choice now that the police are involved." I just listened until I came up with the right response to make her feel better and to sound like I knew what I was talking about. "Girl all you can do is be there for your mom and help her out. Just don't make the same mistakes, take this as a lesson learned." That sounded good. I think I had heard my older sister say something like that before. I was always wiser than my years. I guess that was a good thing. The only problem was I didn't know how to apply it to my own life. Some aspects of my life were a little girls dream and others were a complete nightmare.

"I know what you mean." Kimmy replied. "Rhachelle you want to ride bikes for a little while?" "I can't come outside right now, maybe later." I answered. "Well, I better go. Just come knock on my door if you want to ride bikes later." "Okay Kimmy I will and tell your mom I said hello. Oh and let me know if you want to go to church with me on Sunday."

You see, I was born into a very religious and successful family. My parents were entrepreneurs, Elder and Missionary in the church and from the outside looking in, had it made. I guess you could call us the Jones', because everyone else was trying to keep up with us. Mom didn't hesitate with letting it be known either. She had to have the Mercedes, Cadillac, furs, Louis Vitton, Gucci, Fendi; you name it she bought it. Then she was always having extravagant get togethers at our house. She made sure everyone could see what she had acquired through all of the hard work. I guess I was too young to be impressed, for most of my early years, I just thought it was "life". Like everyone had a housekeeper, attended private school, had tennis lessons at the country club and their parents owned their own business. I guess not.

I guess me being naïve of what everyone else had or the lack thereof, also made me naïve to the fact that some things that went on in my house weren't going on in others.

I was raised in a small town in the Northern part of California. In fact, my family was one of the largest in the town. Everybody knew each other and when we passed one another we politely smiled and bowed our head or just said hello. If I did something wrong and got caught by a neighbor, they would scald me and then also tell my parents. Now every town has its parts that you don't hang out in but for the most part there were no real problems. My family was respected within the community and they knew us by the name we carried. There was so many of us that we were always discouraged to have friends outside of the family. My parents would say, "who needs friends when you have so much family", and that's exactly how it was.

And then there was Sunday morning… "Rise and shine sweet, sweet". Daddy always new how to wake me up, his baby girl. Daddy made sure he kept us in church. Sunday School, YPWW, noon day prayer, you name it we were there. Matter of fact he encouraged a lot of the children in church and he made sure we knew our Bible. Daddy was a teacher, not by profession, but he had a gift to teach. He was patient, easy-going and he showed how much he loved being a father. Everybody knew how daddy was about his girls. "I'm getting up daddy, but I'm so sleepy." "You have to get up baby girl and get dressed so we can get to church", he said.

All the kind words in the world couldn't make up for the woman my daddy shared a room with, my mother, his wife. "I don't know what to wear to church!" I always had some kind of excuse to stay in the bed a little longer. "Wear the dress I just bought you, hanging on the door", replied my mother. "No, I don't like it." Matter of fact, I never liked anything she bought for me to wear. "The dress looks better than you." She replied.

    I don't think anyone was more shocked than I was at my mother's snide remark. She had never taken any of her frustrations out on me. I was always the innocent bystander. I would learn to get use to her putdowns and negativity.

    "Leslie did you hear what mom said to me?" "Yes and what's the big deal, you never want to go shopping with her; I like wearing the clothes she buys", she stated. "I'm not into all that and she knows that", I replied.

You could tell where Leslie's loyalty lied. That's how we were raised. We were each other's greatest enemy. I tried my best not to let it get to me.

My mother new exactly what to say to make it hurt; to make all the love and nurturing from my daddy void. She never offered apologies when she was wrong or when she hurt you to the core. I think from that point on, I had emotionally detached myself from her, my mother, his wife.

She didn't notice, at least I didn't think she did. You see, I was the baby of the family, a splitten image of my mother, as far as complexion goes. We even shared common names Rachel and Rhachelle (pronounced Rah-shell, I was always told it was the Greek spelling for Rachel) but we had nothing else in common so I thought.

I had two older sisters and a brother. My oldest sister, Monique was 14 years older than me and I guess in my mind she was my second mother. She was in highschool by the time I was born. She was quiet, had plenty of friends and had a fight in her. Monique or as I called her, my other mother, was the one who tended to me. I crawled in bed with her when I was sick, tagged along with her and her friends, she combed my hair, when my daddy didn't, and even scolded me when I was wrong. Then there was Anthony, but we called him Tony Junior. He was athletic, played baseball and football. Probably would have gone further in one of them if church didn't conflict with the Sunday games. Really didn't get to know him or bond with him as a brother. He's eleven years older than me. By the time I was old enough to even understand I had a brother he was getting married and moving out. Last but not least, was Leslie. We were closest in age but very different. We went to school together all our lives, we shared a room for a few years but really we were just sisters.

From the outside looking in, life was good. Everyone trusted my parents with their children, since we had all internalized my mother's number one rule. But it wasn't just about what went on, it was about the things that were also lacking.

You see mom always knew what to get to make you forget about the harsh words, or the physical wounds. But she also tried to make up for the fact that she was never around, never combed my hair, never tucked me in bed, never even rubbed my stomach when I was sick. I didn't fall for it, but the rest of them always did.

Leslie always got it the worst. Was it her light complexion or her naturally wavy hair, whatever it was mom sure did try to beat it out of her every opportunity she got. Leslie just seemed to always put up with it. Monique reaped the benefits of the mistreatment as well. She traveled a lot, drove my parents Mercedes, was always in the latest fashions and always had her friends over for sleepovers. I think they enjoyed the clothes, purses, shoes, trips and all the things mom tried to bring to make up for all the grief. I didn't want any part of it.

Though we all had the same mother and father we were all very different. Mom made sure to magnify the differences in order to keep us apart. She played the light off the dark, the younger against the older, boy against girls, father against daughters, always leaving us second-guessing one another. It was like she didn't want us to bond together and retaliate. She was our greatest source of competition. I mean who could compete with a woman who had been Who's Who in California, received one of the highest awards in service throughout the national church, multi-million dollar business and a picture perfect family.

Though I didn't understand my mother's lashing out that morning, I would eventually be able to draw my own conclusion. I didn't have to endure the harsh treatment as a little girl like Monique or Leslie but sometimes I felt like watching it was even worse. I can remember Monique coming home real late after being out with some of our cousins from a birthday party. All I remember is waking up from all the arguing and seeing Monique on the side of her bed, pinned down by mom and being choked. I felt helpless. All I could do was scream, "stop mom, stop". "You're nothing but a tramp. I want you out of my house." My mother's favorite word was tramp. She used it freely when she was upset with one of us girls. "Rachel, leave the girl alone." My father always had to step in and be the voice of reason. That was one of my earliest recollections of the dysfunction.

I decided to go ahead and wear the dress that my mother had gotten me. Her comment made me feel even more uncomfortable in it and it didn't help that it was Youth Sunday and I was on program to sing with the choir. "In his time, in his time, he makes all things beautiful, in his time. Lord please show me everyday as you're teaching me your way, that you do just what you say, in your time."

Yes, I sang in the sunshine band choir. I was actually pretty good. I was a little timid and shy, but church was all I knew and daddy made sure we attended our voice lessons.

Church signified unity, love, joy, peace, faith and family. I guess all the ingredients that were missing at home. Since we spent so much time at church, it was like a home away from home. I never knew life without church. The only problem was that the same facade my mother played outside the church she also played in the church. I guess it was okay for us to look our best at church but sometimes I think she used it as a cover up to the lifestyle she lived in the privacy of our home.

I remember one Sunday, it happened to be right after Christmas, we came to church carrying our new Gucci purses. Yes, mother had bought us Gucci. I was around 6 and Leslie was 10. I remember our Pastor's wife talking to my mother. "Rachel, now don't you think the girls are too young for all that?" She asked. Actually, I think it was more of a statement, than a question. My mother said, "No, the girls got those for Christmas". She politely left it at that and changed the conversation. You see no one knew these were like her symbols of love. You take away the materials things and there went her love.

My mother swiftly climbed the ranks within the church. She was a licensed Missionary; she would have speaking engagements at different churches. I remember being at services supporting her. She could get the attention of the church and deliver a powerful message. She would square her shoulders, stand straight up tall and point her finger, saying, "You have to know, that you know that everything is going to be alright". You could see how God was working and using her in ministry, but sometimes I wondered if she actually believed what she preached. She was always praying. Some of the church mothers and other missionaries would come to the house and they would pray together for hours. I don't know what my mom was praying about but it must have been the businesses and her ministry because family life wasn't changing much.

For a little girl like me it was confusing. I mean we were always singing "Yes Jesus loves me" or "Jesus loves the little children", but if God was so much love and my mom believed in God, why didn't I ever feel like she loved me? It just made me pray harder and keep a tight hold to whatever faith I had. It was during that time that I would begin to think that church was just a show. I mean nothing at home translated to the teaching that I would receive on Sunday morning. From that moment after, that weekly routine became Sunday mourning. I mourned the loss of my childhood, the emotional absence of my mother, the sense of true family but most importantly the understanding of God's love. Church became a constant reminder of all that was truly lacking. I took it very serious and felt the more I emulated my surroundings, the better things would get at home. I think it hurt me more that things didn't change. All we seemed to be living by was a church doctrine. We didn't wear pants, weren't allowed to go to the movies and if you were a boy you were lucky to be able to play sports.

"Hi, little Rachel." Unfortunately, that was what a lot of people at the church called me. "Don't you just look like a little missionary." I made sure I always wore a long skirt or dress and my mom kept me in tights or knee socks. I didn't want anything showing. "I enjoyed your singing this morning. You stay encouraged and keep singing for the Lord." "Thank you Mother Jones." My godmother always encouraged me. I think she saw something in me.

2 NEW LEVELS, NEW DEVILS
~ HOME LIFE

It wasn't soon after the incident with my mother and Monique that Monique decided to go and live with our grandparents. She just couldn't take it anymore. According to Monique, these issues had been going on, I was just too young to know. I could remember some nights being awaken in the middle of the night, to my mother screaming and hollering about the house not being clean or she would be running the vacuum cleaner. Monique would get woken up out of her sleep to clean, even if the housekeeper was coming the very next day. Then my mother would say all types of non-sense while cleaning. I learned to just lie in my bed and pretend to be sleep. Monique did whatever she needed to do to satisfy my mother's demands and prevent there from being any further altercations.

Before Monique moved out she had made a promise to me. It was late one night; Monique had let me come down to her room to chat with her and Leslie. "Hey, little sis! You know I'm moving right?" "Monique, why do you have to go? I don't want you to leave. Who is going to look after me when daddy is gone or is busy? I don't like talking to mom." I had to get it out. I was scared. I didn't want Monique to leave. "I just can't take living here with your mother anymore." She was saying all this as she mixed some household cleaners together in a bottle. I didn't know what she was doing at the moment, but she started to put the bottle with the mixture closer to her nose. "What are you doing Monique?" I asked. "When I'm stressed I inhale this, it just relaxes me. I started sniffing gas first when I was still in high school. I know I need to stop and that's a big reason why I'm going to move. I'm tired of all the fighting and yelling. I'm tired of feeling like nothing." I wish Monique would take me with her. None of us deserved to have to live and deal with my mom. Monique kept talking and her speech became harder and harder to understand. Her eyes started to look weird and I didn't know what was happening to her. I started crying. "Monique, what's wrong with you, are you okay?" "Rhachelle, I'm fine." "Well you don't look fine, you need to stop doing this. It's not good for you." She came over to me and gave me a hug. "I promise I will stop, that's why I need to move." I could barely talk through all my tears. "Please stop Monique, I love you and I don't want anything to happen to you." That was the last night that I got to sleep in Monique's room with her. The next morning her bags were packed and she was moving.

With Monique gone, I relied on my father even more and distanced myself even further away from my mother. He took me school shopping, I confided in him and he protected me from my mother; he was my covering. He was my Valentine, my Easter bunny, my toothfairy and Santa Claus; daddy made sure he played his role in my life. At times he may have thought that he needed to compensate for the lack of presence my mother had, but it didn't show; his love was genuine. I also at times felt bad for daddy when he had to play referee in the midst of my mother's raging fits. She would often get upset when he didn't side with her but her actions were wrong. It started to seem like she would plan her fits around the time that she knew daddy would be gone.

Tony was next in line for all my mother's ill treatment. But its not like he wasn't used to it. Since he was a male it wouldn't get physical as often as it had with Monique, but my mother always found a way to dish it to him to break his will and damage his character. I remember mom throwing his stereo over the balcony and it shattering to pieces. She would even take parts out of his car so it wouldn't start.

"Mom, I have to go to work." "I don't care where you have to go negro. I brought you in this world and I'll take you out." She always made sure to call you a name and she started issues when she knew it wasn't warranted. Fortunately, he made it out the house that day, but he had to leave on foot. My father wasn't home to be the voice of reason, so someone had to be the bigger person and it never was my mother. Tony was lucky though, he didn't have to put up with it for long, he was getting married. Apparently though, the seed of doubt and failure had already been planted in Tony Jr. It would display itself in more ways than one. I still don't know if he actually wanted to get married or if my mother pressured him into it because his girlfriend had ended up pregnant. Either way I suppose it happened, he went through with the wedding and shortly after my nephew was born. My mother appeared to enjoy the life of a grandmother. She absolutely loved shopping for the baby but who would have known that behind the scenes she was pulling the strings to unravel the marriage of the young wed couple. I used to hear my mother on the phone saying, "as long as I'm telling you what's right according to those 66 books, then keep listening. But as soon as a veer away you better take heed." Then you would hear her quoting scriptures from Proverbs. The truth was, she was now in control of two separate households and she enjoyed the power a little too much. Tony worked for our parents and instead of mom making him be a man, she took care of everything else that he couldn't afford. Tony would clock into work and then leave and go to the gym, but he always managed to get a paycheck.

I guess eventually, my mother's instructions veered away from the 66 books in the Bible. One evening, Tony came home to an empty house, no wife or child. That was the last time I saw my firstborn nephew. I was only around 9 years old so I didn't completely understand, I just remember not understanding why I couldn't see the baby anymore. Tony was still young, not even 20 yet, but he didn't come back home, he started living the life of a bachelor again. It was just Leslie and I left in the house. How would the two of us survive all the madness? I continued to keep my distance but Leslie always seemed to put her foot in her mouth. She always had a smart remark or gesture. One Saturday night, we both had went over to my aunt Pam's house to hang out with our cousins. We had actually been together for most of the day. When we got home, all hell would break loose. It started as soon as we opened the door.

"Where have you been" asked my mother. "We were at auntie Pam's" replied Leslie and she pushed past my mother to actually get in the door. Mom kept ranting and raving and Leslie continued to walk towards her room so that there wouldn't be a confrontation. Leslie repeated herself again, "we were just at auntie Pam's house, I don't see the big deal." Leslie should have kept her mouth shut. Before I knew it, my mom had Leslie in a headlock and was pulling her hair. Leslie continued to talk, "mom, are you serious, stop!" "That's your problem, you don't know when to shut up." "Nothing but tramps run the streets this late at night." My mom's favorite word again. Next thing I knew, my mother had picked up a high-heeled shoe and was hitting Leslie over and over again in the head. I stood completely still in the corner, yelling "stop, stop mom". I was scared; I couldn't believe what was happening right before my eyes. My father, I guess heard all the commotion from down stairs and ran upstairs to see what was going on. "Rachel, this doesn't make sense," my dad yelled. I held Leslie's head in my lap as the blood stained my pants. Daddy got my mother to stop but the damage had already been done.

No police called and no doctor's visit. Life went on as if the events from that night were normal. It wasn't normal in my mind but it was too much to discuss outside of the house. I don't know where I packed away the emotions, the fear and even the hatred. But life continued on, the good, the bad and the awful.

The situation reminded me of Kimmy and her mother. If Kimmy's mother hadn't gotten fed up and called the police, I'm sure I would have continued to hear all the bad stories. My dad always assured us he wouldn't leave us, but sometimes I wished he would had left her, my mother, his wife and take us with him. I pictured that life would have been different and possibly better. Kimmy was so happy now and talked about all the changes. It was almost as if I was living my life vicariously through Kimmy. We talked on the phone a lot more and played in the neighborhood. My mom didn't like us having too many friends outside the family, but Kimmy was starting to become a part of my family. I wanted to tell someone about what happened, but instead I just called Kimmy in the morning to see how she and her mom were doing.

"Hello, can I speak to Kimmy?"

"Hey Rhachelle, how is everything going?" "Oh hey Kimmy I didn't recognize your voice." I chuckled. "Things are pretty good. You know my dad just opened up his own church. Things have been a little hectic with that but whatever. How have you been?" "A lot better, the house is a lot quieter, no more fussing, since my daddy is gone. My mom and I have been doing a lot more together and getting some real quality time in. It had been a while since we actually sat down to eat dinner together or even watched TV together. It really makes a difference".

I thought to myself, doesn't that only happen on the Brady Bunch. We never ate dinner together at my house and the only time we watched TV together was when my mom let us pile on her bed.

We all had our own TVs in our room. I remember how excited I was when I first got it, but now hearing Kimmy talk, I wonder if I would have been better off without it. "Well, I'm glad everything is working out. I don't like to see my bestfriend upset. I was just calling to check on you and you know the invitation still stands if you want to come to church." "Alright, thanks for calling. Maybe my mom will let me go to church with you now since she won't have to argue with my daddy about it. I'll let you know, bye." "Bye Kimmy", we hung up with each other. I thought about going in to my mom's room with her to watch television, but I snapped out of it real quick; my mom wasn't Kimmy's mom, who was I fooling.

Church Life

"Heavenly Father we thank you for this day, a day that was not promised. We thank you for waking us up this morning and starting us on our way, clothed and in our right minds. We ask that you bless our coming in and our going out. Touch our minds Lord, your will Lord..."

Daddy always knew how to get a prayer through. He prayed until he touched heaven. He always started service with a soul stirring prayer. See daddy had stepped out on faith and answered the call into the ministry, as a Pastor. Yes I was now a Preacher's kid.

Preacher's kids or "PK's" as they called us, never had it easy; we were always expected to live up to this standard that could never be reached. Because we were always in the spotlight people tried to hold you to it. Church became a separate part of my life. I don't know how to explain it, but since I couldn't figure out how it played a role outside of the building, I couldn't fully commit myself to it anymore. I guess in the words of the church, I couldn't surrender.
We would all attempt to play a role in the church. Leslie learned how to play the drums, lesson's from Tony, Jr didn't hurt, he played when he came to church, Leslie was also the soloist, we were all in the choir, we were janitors, ushers and Sunday School teachers, you name it we did it.

I was finally able to convince Kimmy to start coming to church with me. She loved my daddy, he had always been a father figure to her. "So how did you like church Kimmy?" "Girl I had fun. I like the way your daddy preaches, he makes it easy for me to understand. You know I don't get to go to church often, so when I do go its important I understand. I can't wait to share the message with my mama." At least she enjoyed it, I thought to myself. It was hard for me to look past all the issues at home. I mean how could I surrender to anything, while I was carrying so much baggage.

The church preoccupied a lot of my parents' time. My mother was always planning services and events and my daddy stayed in his word. He had even started attending Bible college. We didn't have a Cathedral, but a lot of people supported my dad's ministry and fellowshipped with us. My mother would organize fundraisers, musicals, appreciations, food drives, toy drives and community picnics. I remember my mother and father came to Leslie and I and asked how we felt about the church hosting a food and toy drive. "We want to do a food and toy drive, for the Community at the church for the holidays, girls", my father stated. My mother continued on, "we wanted to talk to you both and see if you would be willing to give up Christmas to help another family." I don't think either one of us really cared. I knew I didn't. I was over all the gifts and surprises. We answered at the same time, "I don't care."

And so it was. The food and toy drive would end up being a success. The local newspaper ran an article and it even made the news. So many people gathered at the church. Even Kimmy and her family were able to come down to receive a package. Kimmy had told me that her mother had finally left her daddy for good. She said things had been a little rough, but she was glad to have her mother back. "I'm so glad you told me about this Rhachelle. I know my mama was worried about what she was going to do for us on Christmas. Now she doesn't have to worry." "This is what church is all about, showing love and compassion through service to one another." I don't know how I came up with that so quick, but it sounded good so I stuck with it. I mean the Bible does say we are to love one another but does that mean only people we don't know. "Well tell your mom I said hello and Merry Christmas, I better go and help clean up."

More and more people were becoming aware of the little church that was able to give away over 1000 donations to the families in the Community. All the mentions weren't too bad for my mom's businesses either. You could never underestimate her motives.

3 EASYCOME, EASY GO ~ HOME LIFE

After being in business so long, my parents got somewhat comfortable; my mother wasn't going into the office as much but staying at home more. Dad's extra time was focused on ministry and Bible college. Daddy was fully committed to the ministry. However, my mother being at home didn't translate into mother and daughter time, with daddy being away, I would have to learn how and when to reach out to my mom. She suffered from depression; she would hide away in her room for days.

"Rhachelle", she would yell through the house. "Yes." "Can you bring me some water?" "And make sure you put it in a glass and bring a napkin." You see she didn't like plastic, she was demanding and picky, but if I did it right the first time I wouldn't have to deal with her for a while. The problem with that was even though I wasn't dealing with her, I still had to deal with the situation. With her depression came prescription drug use, sporadic shopping sprees, irrational behavior and unexplainable arguments. Her issues were destroying our family and gradually destroying everything that she had worked so hard to achieve.

I didn't understand all the medicine; I didn't even know what it was all for. I just remembered that she always complained about her head hurting or having a migraine. She would even have us rub her head for hours to help with the pain. She saw doctor after doctor and the more of them she saw, the more medication she got. On the other hand, when things were good they were good. I never recalled my mother complaining, arguing or unhappy when we went on family vacations.

I could tell when the finances became an issue though because daddy stopped handing over money so freely. Now I had to beg just to get twenty dollars for the movies. He even asked for his change back sometimes. Our back to school shopping trips to the mall stopped as well. So I did what I saw; I got a job. At fourteen, I started my very first job. I was proud of my job. I worked at a warehouse that distributed nasty magazines. I never told my parents. I mean it wasn't like I had to read them. I just had to take the plastic wrap off of them so that they could be shredded. I got a check every two weeks and I was able to pay for my own shopping and trips to the movies. Work became my security and power. I could now wear pants, since I could afford to buy them.

One thing I noticed it didn't give me the power to change was my mother. I would get home from work and go straight to my room to start my homework. Thursday night was my night to study for my spelling and vocabulary exam. Since daddy attended Bible College on those days, I had to ask my mom for help sometimes. Mom didn't like helping with homework, she lacked the patience, but who else would help me with my spelling test. Leslie was now away at college.

"Mom, can you help me with my spelling test?" "I guess, bring it in here" she replied. I made sure to tell her exactly what I needed to do. "I have to spell the word and give the definition." "Okay, whimsical", she called out. "W-h-i-m-s-i-c-a-l, whimsical", and "the definition", she asked. "Uh, um", it just wasn't coming to me. "Erratic, unpredictable", she blurted out. "You need to study more, here take this back." She handed me my paper. I knew the definition; I had been studying. Maybe she made me nervous. That was the last time I would ask for any help from her. Matter of fact, I wouldn't bother asking her any questions.

Situations that would have sparked a conversation or a discussion in most families only brought on ridicule, judgement and arguments in mine. So just like homework, the birds and the bees was one of those areas that I couldn't go to my mother about. I guess she thought I would just get it. I got it alright. I sought out advice from my friends or just listened in as they discussed, boys, sex, drugs and alcohol. My bestfriend, so I thought, peer pressure, never lied, always told me what I wanted to hear and when she found a new circle of friends, left me feeling used.

I wish Kimmy and I had continued going to school together, but after junior high school her mom decided to send her to public school. My parents refused to even consider letting me go to public school. So I had to make all new friends and try my hardest to fit in. It seemed like everyone knew each other already. I talked to Kimmy almost everyday. We would even meet up sometimes before school and have coffee.

"I'll have a small chocolate mocha," that was my favorite and it was simple. I always liked a lot of whipped cream on top. "I'll have a hot chocolate," Kimmy wasn't into the coffee thing yet, but we would talk and sip until we had to part ways for school.

"How you liking your knew school?" Kimmy asked. I really didn't want to talk about it because I didn't like it. "It's cool I guess, but you know I don't like meeting new people. It takes me a while to get to know people." What I really wanted to say is that, I could no longer hide behind my nice clothes and the fact my parents had money. Everybody I went to school with came from some kind of money and to top It off we had to wear uniforms. So seeing all the similarities that use to make me stand out became the norm. It made it even clearer to me how different my family really was. I mean these kids were actually happy and it wasn't just because they were driving the latest mustang or BMW, they were genuinely happy.

"Rhachelle, hello earth to Rhachelle, snap out of it," said Kimmy. "I guess I was daydreaming. This nice warm coffee is relaxing me. So how is school going for you Kimmy?" "I love it! There are so many different electives outside of my normal classes that I can choose from and then there's tons of extracurricular activities. I'm thinking about trying out to be a cheerleader." "That would be good Kimmy, go for it. Then I could go to the games with you, if my parents let me." "Rhachelle you really think I should?" "Yes girl, do it." I don't know why I through in the comment about going to the games. I knew my parents wouldn't let me. "We better get going before we're both late for school. I can't wait until you tell me about the tryouts, I just know you will make it." I always had encouraging words to give. I just didn't know how to encourage myself. "Thanks Rhachelle, I'll see you later."

Kimmy ended up making it on the cheerleading squad. Since she had never cheered before, she had to go to two practices a day. So instead of meeting up for coffee we just talked on the phone. Just like I had assumed, I didn't get to go to any of the games that Kimmy cheered at. I was glad that I had my job though; at least I had something to keep me entertained.

My coffee buddy soon became Sarah. Not only did we have our morning cup of coffee but also our morning cigarette. Matter of fact my entire circle changed. Nobody knew about this new change. I kept it as my little secret. The fact was I was so alone, insecure and naïve that I went along with anything that seemed cool. It also helped me take my mind off of everything that was going on at home. With things changing so much and so fast at home, I found myself changing at the same pace maybe even a little faster. The cigarettes turned into marijuana, alcohol occasionally and sex. I didn't know much about any of it, I just knew it took my mind off of everything else.

My highschool years were the hardest years of my life. I made sure to keep a job so I could be away from the house as much as possible and have money to spend on myself. See my mother's reckless spending didn't only put a burden on my parent's marriage but it also brought an end to all the success in business. I knew it was coming. I was just glad to be prepared. They lost everything; the cars, the only home that I knew as a child and it seemed like all their friends were gone also.

I remember the day as if it was yesterday. I wish I had been at work but I was home. Maybe that was best because I got to see it with my own eyes and no one could point the finger at the other. "Daddy what's going on, they're taking your car out of the driveway?" I was screaming at the top of my lungs. "Rhachelle, baby girl, calm down. I didn't say anything to you because I didn't want you to worry." I thought to myself, well that still doesn't answer my question. What was going on? My father came to me later on that evening and tried to explain. "Sweet, sweet we have to move. The business hasn't been doing to good and we owe some money that we can't pay." I was dying inside. My life was changing and it was changing fast. I didn't like all the material stuff anyway but this was my home. The place I laid my head, took my first steps, fought with my siblings, played hide n seek and so much more.

The move wasn't as bad as I thought it would be, we ended up moving closer to my school. Daddy was still spending a lot of time away from home. You would think that during these hard times, it would have brought us closer together but it pushed us all further apart. Mom didn't just take her frustration out on me; my daddy often fell subject to the verbal disregard and disrespect. She had always treated him like he was just another employee of hers, but it got even worse. "You're so stupid, that's why we're in the mess we're in now." He didn't offer any comments back. She even at times would try and get physical with him but daddy never lifted a hand to her. I remember Leslie and I begging daddy to leave. "Daddy if you leave, we want to come stay with you", we would both say. But daddy never left, at least not while we were still at home.

Church Life

I didn't have as much time for church anymore, since I started working part time and Sunday seemed to be when I could get most of my hours in. All my work experience had paid off, when I turned sixteen, I applied at the grocery store by our house and I got the job. "Rhachelle, baby girl, time to get up, I can drop you off at work on the way to church." My daddy still knew how to wake me up in the morning. Life was completely different for me than what it had been during my early years. Since I no longer had to go to church, I didn't. My mother had showed me or made me believe that everyone had skeletons and everyone was a hypocrite. So that was one routine that got cancelled. I felt like I could conquer the world and when times got hard I knew how to get on my knees.

I still sang in the choir, when I could make it to rehearsals. I guess that was one of few areas in the church that I didn't have to deal with my mother. One of my favorite songs that we would sing was "Bind us together Lord, bind us together Lord, with chords that cannot be broken, bind us together Lord, bind us together in love."

We sang it at the beginning of rehearsal. One thing no one could deny, was that the little church on the outskirts of town, had a choir that could sing themselves happy.

The church had its faithful few but with so many issues on the homefront, they trickled into the church. My mother seemed to start resenting the church. She would attend, but would drop her head, and wouldn't get behind and support my dad while he was preaching. Not to mention she loved to gossip. She started driving the few members we did have away.

"Girl did you hear about Mother Hangor's daughter?" "They are saying she is pregnant by Elder Laundrie." "It's just a shame before God." These conversations that I overheard made me want to scream. How could people that say they love the Lord talk about folks, instead of pray for them? I mean with all the issues we were having, you would have thought she would have been on her knees praying for even her own family. I was so happy to have a legitimate reason to stop associating with church folks. But would it be to my detriment?

4 A HOUSE DIVIDED CANNOT STAND
~ HOME LIFE

I was finally out of the house. College bound and on a mission, I wasn't looking back. My mother, father and Tony Jr. drove me out to school to get me all settled into my dorm. I had been to San Francisco quite a few times growing up, as a family we all enjoyed Fisherman's Wharf. In the outskirts of the City sat a school plagued by a cloud of fog, but surrounded by the best neighborhood full of life. San Francisco State University would be where I started my educational experience. It was close enough to home in case there was an emergency yet far enough for me to learn some independence and mature as a young woman. My roommate was one of my fellow classmates in highschool so we would get the opportunity to tackle the world together. We had both lived a very sheltered life growing up so a lot of our experiences together would be a first.

Kiran was Indian, from the Middle East. She understood the strict rules that our parents had taught us and believed that we would continue practice in their absence. We broke them all. "Rhachelle do you want to go to this party that some of the kids in my class are throwing on the beach?" I knew that basically meant Rhachelle will you drive. It seemed like I was the only freshman that actually had a car on campus, so I quickly became the designated driver. "Sure, I'll go but everyone that rides with me will need to give some gas money." "Okay no problem, I think it will just be two more people with us." Our first crazy party experience was crazy. We were out in the middle of nowhere, loud music, and even bright strobe lights. I found it quite entertaining at first. I sat back and laughed, it was hilarious. "Kiran, why are all these people acting so weird?" "I was wondering the same thing, but someone just told me that they are on ecstasy." I could not believe what she had just said. I had never been around it or people that were on it. I think we both felt the same way. We looked at each other and we both knew the next move. "Are you ready?" I asked. "I sure am." That was one thing I liked about my roommate we both had our limits. We trusted each other's instinct.

On the weekend we would drive home together. I would drop off at home and enjoy her mother's homemade Chai tea. We would sit and talk and laugh until I'd get ready to go to my parent's house. Kiran's relationship with her mother reminded me of Kimmy's and her mother. Something I knew nothing about. On our rides home Kiran would share with me some of the things that concerned her about her parents. "You know Rhachelle, I like to come home a lot because I worry about my mom." "Why do you worry about your mother so much Kiran?" "It's my dad, when he gets drunk and stressed he takes it out on her. My mother always acts like things are okay, but I tell her to leave. She won't leave though." Our conversations were so familiar to me. I always found myself repeating the same things that I had told Kimmy. "Well all you can do is be there for her. Learn from her mistakes and try not to make the same ones." A lot of times, I was speaking more to myself than to my friends but I still didn't know how to apply it to my own life. "I'll call you on Sunday before I come to get you.

Have some fun with your mom. Tell her I loved the tea." "Thanks, Rhachelle. I'll tell her and I'll see you Sunday."

The first semester of my freshman year, I went home every time I got a chance. I guess I was home sick. I usually just spent time with my dad or my cousins when I went home. Kimmy had went out of State to go to school. She attended Southern University in Louisiana. Sometimes I wished I had went out of State for school with her. As soon as I would get home, I would realize why I had been so excited to be away at college. I always knew where to find my mother, held prisoner in her bed. We would chat a little bit and then I would just spend the rest of my time watching TV with my dad or gone.

"Daddy what are you watching?" "I'm just checking my stocks." I always remembered seeing the numbers move across the bottom of the screen but daddy never taught me much about the stocks. I didn't mind it though I just enjoyed being in his presence. "Daddy when did Tony Jr. move in?" "Oh your mother told him he could come and stay. I don't know what his problem is and your mother never listens to me. I'm ready for him to leave." I could tell by daddy's voice that he was serious and irritated. "Well now I don't have a room. I guess I won't be coming home as much anymore." He shook his head and sighed, "I know, sweet, sweet, I told your mom that but its like she doesn't hear anything." For some reason my mother had always rescued Tony Jr. when things got rough. He never had to tough it out as a man. If you asked me I think he never really believed in himself. I guess we were a lot a like in some of the worst ways possible. We doubted our abilities and therefore we never tried or followed through with anything because of the fear of failing.

Sunday came fast. I woke up early and got all my things together so I could head back to school. I didn't see any point in attending church. I headed to Kiran's house to pick her up and we headed back to the City. "So how was your weekend with your family Kiran?" "It was pretty good, my cousin got married; I got to see a lot of my family. Oh yeah and my mom made sure to make you some Indian food, so we can stock our refrigerator." I loved the Indian food Kiran's mom would cook. Neither one of use liked eating in the cafeteria. As a matter of fact, we hadn't eaten in it our entire first semester. "Sounds good, my dad made me some food also, so we will have plenty." My dad would always make my favorite, spaghetti. He made sure to send plenty so that it would last a couple of days. Kiran and I had gotten spoiled and eating out at different restaurants had gotten expensive.

I knew things had changed even though I wasn't at home anymore but daddy never even hinted around about leaving. I stopped spending as many weekends at home and would just find things to do with my friends. I would call home from college and my daddy wouldn't be home. Usually he was still at the church or at Bible college. My mother knew when I was calling, that it wasn't to speak with her. She would just say, "Hello, you want to speak to your father?" "Yes, is he home?" Was always my response. I can remember my freshman year when I had made the same call. Daddy hadn't made it home from church so I decided to talk to my mother. Classes were getting harder and I was under a lot of pressure. "Mom, I just can't do this anymore." I just needed some encouragement. I'm sure not having any sleep accounted for my hysteria. Her reply, "drop out then." I couldn't believe the words that had just been spoken. Then I thought, that was typical of her, my mother, his wife.

That's all it took for me to stop talking to her, at least as it related to college. I worked really hard in college. I always tried to involve myself in community service while carrying a full load and also pledged my sorority my sophmore year. After all these years, I had found a sisterhood; Alpha Kappa Alpha, Eta Sigma Chapter, people(sisters, sorors) that were more like me than my own flesh and blood. They pushed me, encouraged me, inspired me and kept my spirits high when I should have been breaking to pieces. During that same semester, I would visit my mother in rehab over my Thanksgiving break, another skeleton I would make sure to stash away in the closet. I soon replaced my family with my sorority. I only allowed my father into my new world. I made college my refuge. I traveled, stayed involved in activities and maintained my focus in my studies. I guess since my dad saw that I was okay and had totally committed myself to school, he could moved on.

    I stopped coming home completely, except for Christmas. Thanksgiving I spent with Kimmy and her family in Louisiana. I was so proud of Kimmy she was doing well away from home. I ended up not even going home after the completion of my freshman year. I ended up moving into my first apartment with some friends. Kiran and I had stopped talking because of her boyfriend. He was somewhat controlling and had stalker tendencies. I remember the night he called her and threatened to kill himself if she broke up with him. Like always, I tried to give her the best advice. "Kiran you need to leave him alone. He is not right for you. You need to focus on school and he tries to interfere too much. You've been staying out late, coming in drunk and then he calls you all night as if he doesn't trust you." "I know Rhachelle, but I'm not going to leave him." That night he left repeated messages on her phone as if he was going to kill himself. Then sometime in the middle of the night he showed up at our dorm room. He looked disheveled and disturbed. I never wanted to look into his face again and since Kiran wouldn't leave him. I decided to move out.

I wasn't the only one that had moved or quit coming home. Daddy had been gone for two weeks before my mother even noticed. You see she had driven him away. You would think that with all the praying, the church conventions and fancy clothes, she would have gotten her act together, but no change. I was so upset. I couldn't believe it. Down through the years, my father had been the blame for all my mother's issues. Her entire family needed a scapegoat and my daddy became the target. He hadn't created all of her issues, maybe not even some of them, but it was easier to point the finger.

Daddy just couldn't take it anymore. He had his own health problems. Daddy had underwent three open heart surgeries, two in my lifetime. He had terrible arthritis and had been considered disabled since his early twenties. He didn't need the stress or drama that my mother always fueled. It wasn't that he didn't care about my mother anymore, but it was time that he started caring a little more about himself.

I wish I had gotten to talk to him before he left. I wouldn't have tried to convince him to stay, but I would have told him I understood and didn't love him any less for doing so. I know daddy loved church and the ministry but everything going on at home just didn't coincide with his biblical teachings. Tony Jr. had gotten himself in a rut and my mother always came to his rescue. He had moved in with his girlfriend and my nephew and had another baby on the way. Daddy was against him staying at the house but my mom never let daddy have the final say so. Tony Jr. was actually staying in what was supposed to be my room. College was my saving grace. I would find out about daddy leaving the summer after my Sophmore year.

I guess daddy had been contemplating leaving for quite some time. My freshman year in college, my grandfather, my mother's father, passed away. My daddy said that he had advised my daddy to leave my mother or else she would kill him. He didn't mean he would die at her hand but the stress on his heart would kill him. I blamed her, my mother, now his ex-wife. I couldn't fault him for leaving. I would've been gone. I was staying with my sister Monique and her husband for a little while until I got my own place. I cried and cried and cried. No more calling home to speak to daddy. He didn't want to be contacted. For months, the only way I could reach him was by paging him and hoping he would call back. I would page and wait. It killed me, my daddy, best friend and biggest fan.

My sorority became my substitute for everything, my family, church, entertainment, etc. If there was one thing my mother taught me, it was compassion. I volunteered as often as I could with my sorority, compassion seemed to become my substitute for church; It filled the void. I volunteered with children, fed the homeless with my sorority sisters, but in times of trouble I always knew where to turn. My mother had engrained in me the importance of prayer. The one thing I didn't know how to do was surrender. Surrendering would involve me letting go, tearing down the wall I had built a long time ago and ultimately accepting my past. So instead of surrendering, I went from relationship to relationship, surrendering my flesh but believing I was still in control of my soul. I didn't realize that I was actually losing bits and pieces of my soul which were being polluted by the false love. The decent relationships I ran from because I couldn't connect with them because deep down inside I didn't know how to love. I ignored them, made them feel unimportant but at the same time I gave my body away to them. How I felt on the inside was being demonstrated on the outside and no one saw through it all.

I continued on with school, accumulating baggage and hanging more and more skeletons in my closet. I even switched my studies from Biology to Psychology. Maybe I would be able to relate to all the dysfunction that had been buried.

Church Life

I attended church every once in a while. I just felt awkward going. Everyone had known my parents and I didn't want to be questioned. I wouldn't join a church, just fellowship. I remember one Sunday, I attended Good Samaritan with one of my sorors. After the service was over, the Pastor came up to me and said, "Smith, right?" All I could think was wow, how did he know my name. I nodded and shook his hand. That did it for me. I would just go to church when I was down and out, cry all the hurt out, give an offering, sing some songs and then back to my life. I guess I hoped for some change to happen but I really didn't know what it all meant anymore; nothing about God and church made any sense. That probably sounds crazy since church was all I new, but it was the application that I had been missing.

5 THE REAL WORLD

I would go on to complete college. Daddy and I chatted every now and again. I don't even recall speaking to my mom very often after the divorce. But of course she wanted to take all the credit for me completing school. She showed her support by throwing me a graduation party.

I had to invite my parents to two separate graduations. My mother attended my Black graduation and my father, the University graduation. I was so glad he had attended. He was the one that pushed me and supported me. Monique never made it and neither did Leslie. I wasn't shocked. I guess the graduation and/or I didn't matter to them. I couldn't imagine them being jealous. We all were given an option to attend college expenses paid; daddy was a veteran. Either way it went that seed jealousy had been planted in us years ago. Anthony attended both ceremonies, but deep down, no one else mattered but daddy.

I had never had a big party before, not even for my birthday. It was nice being the center of attention and being surrounded by family and friends. I would have given everything for daddy to be there. He had given me all my inspiration; I couldn't take all the credit. My mother basked in it though; I couldn't blame her. I was the first to obtain a Bachelor's degree. However, it wouldn't fill the void.

I didn't realize how much being done with college would change my life. There was no home or real family to go back to. My mom, now his ex-wife was forced to move into a one-bedroom apartment. That meant I had to keep my apartment and find a job to make sure the bills were paid. I managed for a while but life would take a sharp turn. I was fortunate to find a decent paying job after I graduated. I was working in my field with severely emotionally disturbed (SED) adolescents. I loved my job and now I was actually getting paid for my words of wisdom, although I still didn't know how to apply them to my life. I worked the graveyard shift and any other shift that needed to be filled. I had a plan. I would take a semester off from school and return in the Spring to continue on with my plans to go to medical school. I enjoyed the time off from school, but I still stayed connected. One of my line sisters was on the 5-year plan and she was set to graduate with one of my neos.

I worked throughout the next fall and continued to interact with my Sorors. I guess you could call me the great entertainer; I loved having get-togethers at my place. We had plenty of girl's nights. I completed my applications to Long Beach State University and played the waiting game, but it wasn't so bad because I stayed busy. I knew I would get in; I had completed my undergrad with a pretty decent GPA. So I shifted my attention to just finding housing, I had enough of the dorms and just wanted to find a decent place in the City. Half way through the fall semester was over I found out that I had gotten accepted. So I planned a roadtrip. My sorority sister lived in Los Angeles, so I would drive her home for the holidays and begin my search for a place and a job. Finding a place wasn't that hard, the job on the otherhand would present the greatest obstacle. I just needed a part-time job so that I could meet the income guidelines for my lease. I was still eligible to receive my GI bill allowance every month that I had gotten during my undergrad. I tried to convince the leasing agent that with my student loans and my monthly allowance, that I would be able to pay my rent, but it was a no go.

I made one last attempt. I went to my mom. I thought she would be excited to help since she had been so excited about my graduation. "Mom, I can't get my apartment for school because I can't find a job. I know I can afford the rent because I get my monthly allowance and I will be getting financial aid. Do you think you could help me with securing the place?" "Why don't you ask your father? Did you ask him to help?" The biggest slap in the face that I had ever gotten without leaving a handprint. My father had made sure that I had gotten through four years of undergrad. Where had she been that entire time? She gladly took all the credit for it but she was blatantly refusing to help me now. "Mom, daddy helped me for the past four years and its not like I need any money, I just need a co-signer." "Well, I don't know what to tell you." I can't say that my determination would have continued on had her response been different but I easily took on the attitude of defeat and gave up.

All my plans to continue on with school fell through; I soon found myself expecting a child, receiving a wedding invitation and losing my best friend, my daddy for good. I don't know if I was ready for a child and motherhood but I desperately needed to be loved and have a family. I guess I thought a family could replace all my dreams. He must have seen all my insecurities because he took advantage the first chance he got. Everybody warned me but I didn't listen. David, no ambition, into everything but the right thing and still waiting on God to change him approached me. His favorite line "If God can't change, I can't be changed". He never even tried. I couldn't believe he had even tried to step to me and like every other time before, I didn't shoot him down. He had watched me go through all four years of college. He also saw me grow up in the church. Yeah, he was always hanging around the church but being in the church and the church in him was a different story. He knew his Bible and that intrigued me. How could this bad boy quote the word, believe in the word but not live by the word. I saw all the red flags. I had been the one advising all my friends about this same type of guy. I guess I would have to learn it for myself, the hard way. I think we were both crying out for something, maybe the need to belong. I didn't realize then, but he was a reflection of me at that point in my life. I had attracted who I had become, carrying baggage never looked well on anyone. I would end up carrying a lot more than baggage.

"Are you sure that's my child?" He asked. "What do you mean am I sure? You mean all this time we've been together day in and day out and you're questioning me?". My mind told me to end it, which I did, but my heart would fail me over and over again. "So are you going to keep it or what?" "What do you mean, am I going to keep the baby? I'm a grown woman, with a college education, I have no reason to have an abortion." He kept pressuring me, continuously pressing the issue.

"Smith, is there a Smith here?" Two weeks had went by and I gave in. I made the appointment at the clinic. I arrived on time. I had went to David's house to pick him up but he wasn't home. I received a call from David. He told me he was at another girl's house. "So are you coming, I'm here? I went by your grandmother's they said you weren't there." "No, I'm chillin right now." I couldn't believe him, was he serious. How could someone be so cold? I don't even remember saying bye; I just hung up. "Smith, last call." They were calling my name again. I had never been through this before and to go through it alone would be crazy.

Church Life

Dealing with David off and on again, I had no choice but to seek refuge in the church. It seems like every time I attended the message was directed to me. I would sit towards the back and silently cry the entire service. I wanted that happiness and joy that everyone else appeared to have. I just didn't know how to get it. I was attending church, just like when I was little. I would feel good while I was there but would be a mess once I left. What was I missing, what wasn't I getting?

6 MOTHERHOOD

I would endure the next 8 months alone. Actually my mother stepped up to the plate but at any time I could be subjected to being called out of my name. I had decided I would rather raise a child alone than to deal with the guilt and pain of having an abortion. David didn't call, he just gave my number out to other girls to harass me. He even sent girls into my job. He once told me, "all I remember is that you always had money". Well I would become his ATM for the next 7 years. The relationship was awful and every time we got back together, I felt like I lost a piece of me and not to mention ended up pregnant. In 7 years, we managed to have five children that I had to learn to love, nurture and guide and I even let him convince me to abort our second child. Those that I met that didn't know me before David believed we were married. It helped ease some of the embarrassment. I actually spoke highly of him in public. But I had a bigger issue, you see all those years I had shut my mother out, I never got to see how a mother, mothered. All I knew was how to ridicule, scream, fuss, ignore and make up for it all with materialistic gifts. I also learned how to belittle, control, manipulate, disrespect, condescend and blame a man for every wrong or mistake I managed to commit. Now I'm left putting the pieces back together and trying to figure out how "u" interrupted my Sunday morning.

    I didn't understand how someone could be so evil. I had only experienced this hate from one other person. None of my past relationships had ever been this bad. I had slowly accepted the love that I had been taught which displayed itself as hate. I tried to make the most out of the situation I was in. I worked and even went back to school. Life wasn't great but this is how I knew to keep going. I worked throughout the entire pregnancy. I remember the day I had my daughter as if it were yesterday. It was early Christmas morning. We had just gotten in from Christmas ever dinner at my aunt's house. It seemed like I had just layed down and my stomach started bothering me. I thought I was hungry so I headed straight to the kitchen for some food. That wasn't it. It was two o'clock in the morning and I didn't want to have to wake up my mama, but I did. "Mom, my stomach is hurting." "What do you mean its hurting?" Maybe she had forgotten I was pregnant. "Umm, hello I think I'm in labor, I keep having these sharp pains." She sat up in the bed, got up and got herself together. "Mom what are you doing?" "I'm cooking the string beans for Christmas dinner. They shouldn't take too long. Its going to be a while before that baby gets here." I couldn't believe her, but it would be another 12 hours until my bundle of joy made his arrival.

My mom acted like she was uncomfortable in the delivery room, offering no real comfort or even small talk. David would never arrive and not even make a phone call. He wouldn't see his son until after a week of him being in the world. It bothered me but I didn't let it show. I didn't want anything or anyone to interfere with the happiness my new bundle of joy was bringing.

I continued to make progress with my life. I eventually got my own place, enrolled in another semester of school and committed myself to attending full time. David started coming around to see his son more often. My mother was helping out with babysitting, staying at my apartment with me during the week. David would consistently come by over the weekend unless I was spending time with friends. It seemed to be a good balance but I didn't see David trying to sneak his way back into my life; I was totally blindsided.

One weekend while David was spending some time with the baby and I, he asked, "why don't I start watching the baby, so your mother doesn't have to stay out here with you?" It made sense, my mother lived forty-five minutes away and I could tell she thought I was taking advantage or didn't appreciate what she was doing. We got into it occasionally so I thought a break could be good for both of us. My response should have been why don't you look for a job so we can put the baby in daycare. But I would once again fall for the deceit. Before I knew it, he had moved in and brought his lifestyle with him. I would soon fall back into old habits, smoking weed and drinking. I was use to the occasional weed smoking but daily was a bit much. He was convincing me to spend large sums of money. My friends were getting pushed further and further away and so was my family. Even though I was the independent one, he was revealing the unsure, dependent and insecure person that he could manipulate.

I would come home from school and work to find different people in my house getting high, with my son in the next room. Before I could even get in the house "can you take me to my grandmother's house?" See David wanted to act like he was playing daddy by day but wanted to hang out all night. I caught onto the game and eventually put the baby in daycare at my school. It worked out much better and I didn't have to worry, but getting rid of David was another story.

David would still come around. I mean he was a user and charmer and he took full advantage. I remember I had, had enough of all the games and lies. I refused to give him anymore money. "C'mon if you just loan me five-hundred dollars I can get this motorcycle and start working. I promise as soon as I get my first paycheck I'll pay you back." It sounded good, but all so familiar. "I am not giving you a dime David." He picked up our son and said "I guess I'll see you when you're 18 and I'll just have to explain to you the situation then." I was hysterical, did our child just become his pawn. "Are you serious? You are saying you are not going to be in her life if I don't give you the money." He didn't back down. But why did I care, why was it so important to keep someone so terrible around. I made him sign a contract and gave him the money. The contract would mysteriously disappear, but as I had done before in times of trouble, I began to pray.

I don't even know if my prayer was specific enough; I just new that I needed a way out of the situation by any means. I decided to get a roommate. I really didn't need the second bedroom; the baby was still sleeping in the room with me. I enjoyed having a roommate, it offered somewhat of a distraction. The only thing is David got even slicker. He figured if he couldn't beat it, join it, so he made a point to befriend her. He even made it a point to tell me while we were alone that he thought she might like him. He made sure that I trusted no one and that I remained isolated. Then the day of confrontation came. "Tracy, asked me to help her move." Why was David the one telling me she was moving? I had let Tracy stay with me and we had never discussed her paying any rent. "What do you mean? She didn't tell me she was moving." I don't know if I was more irritated about not knowing or the fact that she had asked him to help her before speaking to me. I probably should have waited until I had calmed down to confront her but I didn't. "Tracy, did you ask David to help you move?" "Yes, I didn't think it would be a problem with you, I offered to pay him," she sounded innocent. I guess I should have processed everything before proceeding with the conversation. "Well you should have asked me first, instead of going behind my back. Looks like you're going to have to ask one of those mexicans on the street, cause he ain't doing it." I just kept going on and on. "How you going to come up in my house and then go behind my back? You haven't even given me a dime for staying here." Why was I saying all this? Fact of the matter was David had been staying also and wasn't paying and he had also moved his cousin in. Another friend lost and for what?

My prayers wouldn't stop there. If I couldn't bring someone into the situation to strengthen me, then maybe I just needed a way out of it completely. David was bringing more weed into the house and had now let it be known that he used cocaine. I'll never forget the night, "the man" as he called him, knocked on my door. It was like the devil had appeared in the flesh. I was a nervous wreck. I had never used anything harder than weed and I wasn't about to start now. That was enough for me. I called David's mother and let her know what I had witnessed and I continued praying. It wasn't long before my prayers were answered.

I arrived home from school the next day with an eviction noticed taped to me door. I had paid my rent; I didn't know what was going on. "David, my landlord put an eviction notice on my door. It says admitted use of a controlled substance and domestic altercation. What is this all about?" He didn't even try to get a story together. "My cousin said he had been smoking in the house and the landlord came to the door and he told her." I couldn't believe this, where was I suppose to go? I had no place or no one. I could ask my mom. I didn't let it bother me too bad. All I could think about was, maybe this was God's answer to my prayer.

With everything that I was going through, I had forgotten about the wedding invitation that had come in the mail. It had been 4 years since my parents divorced. My relationship with my father still wasn't back to how it use to be and I hadn't even met his soon be bride. I didn't appreciate finding out about her through a wedding invitation; I hadn't even considered attending.

"Hello, Rhachelle," it was my daddy calling. "Yes." "What happened to you, you missed the wedding." Did he really want to know why I didn't attend? I think he would have been upset if I was getting married and he found out when the invitation came in the mail. I let him have it. "You could have at least called and introduced me to her before you sent me an invitation. How can I support something when I don't even know the other person? You obviously weren't concerned about how I felt, so I didn't think it would matter that I hadn't attended." I didn't even pause to let him interject. I was furious. "Baby girl, I'm happy and I didn't know how you would feel and I didn't want any issues from your mother." He always used my mother as an excuse, I guess he forgot that was his ex wife. "You know I don't get along with mom, so why would I even talk to her about you." This conversation was going nowhere. I guess all those years of him being unhappy in an attempt to keep our family together had in the end made him a little selfish. There really wasn't much more for me to say. I just wanted to get off the phone. "Well dad, I'm going to let you go. Love you." "Love you too baby girl, bye." "Bye daddy." Our conversations became less frequent and more distant. I guess I pushed him away also to deal with the pain. Not realizing that all those years he had been my covering. I was now left with no covering and no real understanding of love.

I had to get my head together. So much was happening and so fast. I was returning to the home of my mother, I was expecting yet another child with David and I felt like I had no one. The embarrassment, shame and fear was unbearable and my mother served as a constant reminder of all the mistakes I had made. I tried my hardest to deal with it all and continued to make school my escape.

7
A LEOPARD DOESN'T CHANGE ITS SPOTS

I moved back in with my mother and David went back to his mother's house. It seemed like once the environment changed, David did as well. He was very supportive throughout this pregnancy. I guess he felt like he had a lot of making up to do. He cooked dinner for me a few times per week, he had even gotten a decent job and he did all this without us living together. "Babe, do you want me to cook for you and your mother this evening?" He always tried to make me whatever I was craving. This pregnancy wasn't like the first one, I was carrying the baby low and I wasn't too comfortable on my feet. "Just the usual, some chicken wings, yams and macaroni and cheese. " I'm sure he didn't think I appreciated it but at the same time I deserved it. I didn't know if his actions were truly sincere or if he just wanted to stay on my good side so that he could use my car. I think I ignored all the possible negative reasons and just focused on how I was finally being treated, like he cared.

David would drive me to and from school. He kept my car clean. He seemed to be doing everything that a good man would do. I knew it would take him some time before he would be able to buy a car and with another baby on the way we needed to save all the money we could. I was only working part time and school took up the rest of my time. Our oldest son would turn two after the baby was born. We had our hands full but we were making it work.

I tried to keep my distance from my mother because sometimes she could get vindictive and it would come out of nowhere. When it got too crazy I would just have David come and pick me and the baby up; we would go to his mother's house. I didn't appreciate being called out of my name or made to feel like nothing. I was doing a lot better than a lot of people in my situation. It wasn't like I couldn't move and get my own place I chose not to so that I could save up and finish my post baccalaureate courses. "Rhachelle, I don't know why you let that negro use your car all the time. It wouldn't be me."

All I could think is that it wasn't her and she didn't pay my car note. "Mom what is the problem now? You go from one thing to the next." "I'm just saying and if you don't want to hear it you can get out. Go lay up in his mother's house." She always tried to get rid of me. She always acted like she didn't want me around. Why was I always made to feel like a burden when I did so much? I kept groceries in the house, I watched her foster children when she went to her meetings, I even cooked dinner, at least when David wasn't around. I would go back and forth between my mom and being with David at his mom's house for the entire 9 months.

Our second son would be born on Thanksgiving Day. We had covered two major holidays. David was right there but none of his family came. My family left Thanksgiving dinner to come welcome our newborn son. I tried to act like it didn't bother me, that his family didn't come but it seemed to shed light on the fact that deep down inside our relationship was a joke. "David, why didn't you family come to the hospital?" I asked. "I told them not to." He replied. Why would he tell them not to come? I felt like my position with my family was changing because of this pathetic relationship and neither my children nor I were accepted into his. So

I bounced back and forth, depending on who was hurting me the least at that particular time. "Why would you tell them not to come? If it was anybody else in your family having a baby everybody would be right there." I was upset but more so hurt. I thought things were getting better between us but this move he pulled shed light on a lot of things.

We spent three days in the hospital and finally it was time to go home. I was at the hospital alone with my baby. David had to go into work and had made the mistake of giving my key to my mom. I could always count on my mom to stay true to her character. I had to call her though, how else would we get home. "Mom, I don't have a way home from the hospital. The car is here but you have the keys." I didn't expect that to turn into an argument. "I sure do have the keys, that negro don't need to keep driving around in your car." All I could think about was that this was not the time. I probably would have agreed with her if she didn't treat me as bad as he did. "Mom, the point is how am I going to get home and who is going to pick us up?" I didn't want to raise my voice but could she at least reason with me. "Bye, Rhachelle." All I heard was the dial tone. Bye, was she serious, why did she hang up on me? I wasn't in the mood for her games at all. I had to call Monique to let her know what was going on. "Monique, I am up at this hospital stranded. Your mother took the keys to my car from David and won't come up here to get me. I was discharged a while ago." I didn't even give her a chance to ask any questions. "You gotta be kidding me?" I could tell in her voice that she was upset. "I'm on my way." Monique didn't play and it had been a while since she exchanged words with my mom.

I waited patiently. I made sure everything was ready. The baby was wrapped up and sitting snug in the carseat when Monique arrived. "You read? This doesn't make any sense. I had to get up out of my bed and drive way out here to pick you up." Monique lived about 25 minutes outside of the City. "Monique, I don't know what her problem is. She took the keys from David and wouldn't give them to anyone else or just come and get me herself." I think the more I talked the more upset Monique got. "Let's go. We are going to her house. If she starts acting crazy you are just going to have to come and stay at my house." It wasn't a bad plan since my oldest daughter was already there with her. In times like these

Monique always came through, that's why I always considered her my other mother. She always did what my mom should have done.

Nothing could ever be simple or rational with my mom. When we got to the house all the lights were on and my mom's car was in the driveway. I went to the door and rang the doorbell. At first, no answer; I rang it again. Still no answer, so I called the house phone. "Hello." "Hello, mom can you open the door, I need my car keys." She finally opened the door. Monique didn't hold back. "What is the problem? I had to get up out of my bed, come all the way out here for this non-sense. Give me this girl's keys." You see all those years my mom had treated Monique wrong and made her play the role of mama was all coming back. Monique didn't back down anymore and she said exactly what was on he mind. I don't think my mom was prepared for that. Instead of my mom handing over the keys she pushed through us. Now we were all in the front yard trying to convince her to give me my keys. Anthony even showed up. My mom raced through the front lawn through something across this street into a neighbor's yard and ran to her car. We all thought it was my keys but it was dark outside and no one could see or even hear where they had dropped. "Where is she going?" I yelled at the top of my lungs. She had turned from the driveway onto the lawn and drove off the curb instead of backing her car out of the driveway. We all jumped into the car to follow her. Me and my newborn were in a highspeed chase. She led us all to the police station. She started banging on the front door and yelling, "They're trying to kill me, help, help." I was mad but I wasn't that mad. She had brought this on herself. We weren't trying to harm her; I just wanted my keys. "Mom, are you serious? All you had to do was give me my keys. This is ridiculous. You always have to start some drama." The officer had to stand in between us. Of course he initially sided with her since there was so many of us but once he talked to us separately he understood the issue. I still didn't end up with my key but the police advised me not to stay with my mom. I had no place to go with my newborn baby. Fortunately, Monique said I could stay with her for a few days until things cooled off.

    This would continue to be the cycle that I lived; I would fight with my mom, go back to David, fight with David and end up back with my mom. The emotional and verbal abuse that I would endure made me feel at times that I no longer wanted to live. I didn't owe either of them anything. It wasn't like David and I were even together. He was back to running the streets, and he should have been too busy to keep an eye on me. He controlled me with his lies, he blamed me for his faults and he made sure to remind me that no one was going to want me; I was stupid, all used up and crazy. Wow his words weren't too far from the words that my mom had led me to believe, maybe they were both right.

8 SOUL TIES ~ SOUL CRIES

The relationship between my mother and I was still somewhat distant and it always felt forced. Even after our big blow up, I ended up going back to live with her. I had no choice, two children, part-time work but I had finished up with all my college courses. I didn't know which way my life was headed. I felt like I had given up on all my dreams but more so I had given up on life. I was in need of some sort of parental guidance and support, so I reached out to the one that was available, even though her availability was only her physical presence. She still refused to relate to me as her daughter. When I went to her with my stories or issues, she always just said, "I could tell you a few things. You wouldn't believe some of the things I went through." All I could do was think that maybe if she talked and shared with me some of the obstacles she went through, I would not have had to experience them myself or at least believe I could get through my own. Why was she holding on to so much pain and hurt? Was that her idea of being strong? The more she held her skeletons in her closet, the less I trusted her with mine. See I learned that whenever I shared anything with her, I had to be prepared at anytime for it to be thrown back in my face. I would crawl on my mother's bed and just start conversing with her about life. "Mom, I can't believe everything that I'm going through. I don't understand how David could be so cruel. I thought that he was really trying to do better after we had Willie" She never hesitated to interject while I was talking about my life. "A person will only do to you what you allow them to do. You just need to leave that Negro alone. He's a bum, ghetto and a liar." I often thought that she didn't get that by her saying all those nasty things, that she was putting me down and my children. At least that's how I felt; I mean let me be the one to say the insults. It didn't make it any better that she would frown up her face in disgust when she even mentioned him. A lot of times it made me feel like she was even looking down on me. I understood I made a bad choice, but did it lessen me as a person? If that was the case, then David had won and his mission had been accomplished. So instead of me just dealing with the issue and getting over the relationship I continued to cover it all up. I was not just struggling emotionally but also in every other aspect of my life.

I found a good paying job, moved out of my mother's house and was once again doing all right for myself. I continued to prove to myself that life was better without David but for whatever reason he kept entering my life and at the wrong times. The soul ties were impossible to sever on my own and my faith was lacking in so many areas that I couldn't even pray them away. I found myself again working just to take care of all the bills, while David blue off every penny he earned. I was working full time and also tutoring on the side. Not to mention our baby wasn't even a year yet. My body just couldn't take it anymore. I woke up in the middle of the night and realized I couldn't even lift my arms. I felt like I was starring in my own nightmare. I crawled my way over to the phone and called my mother. "Hello, mom?" "Yes. Is this Rhachelle or Leslie?" She always got our voices confused. "It's Rhachelle. Mom it feels like my shoulder is dislocated, my body is aching and I can barely move." "What's wrong with you, what happened?" "I have the chills, I think I'm running a fever but I'm in so much pain." I knew I had to call my mom because David wouldn't make sure I was okay. He hadn't even made it in with my car. "Do you think you can drive over here?" She asked. "No, David is gone in my car and I'm in too much pain." "Well as soon as he gets there you have him bring you over here." Now one thing I could count on was that my mom would take care of me when I wasn't feeling well. She didn't do it when I was a child, but she was stepping up now.

I didn't know what was going on at the time and neither did the doctors, but God had provided me with another way of escape. I was in and out of the hospital for six weeks. I was being given morphine and every other pain medication you could think of. At times I couldn't even walk. One doctor wanted to diagnose me with rheumatoid arthritis, the next with fibromyalgia. I was in and out of the hospital but it was enough time for God to have some alone time with me. I found myself watching some of the evangelist on television and my spirit was once again being lifted. Since I was staying with my mother, David didn't have as much access to me. He didn't like that, the more time we spent apart the less influence he had on me. I just hoped I wouldn't wear out my welcome with my mother.

I was finally diagnosed with the Epstein Barr Syndrome, which causes chronic fatigue. My doctor told me my body was just exhausted and was shutting down. She also said that I would be on and off a job for the rest of my life. I ended up losing the job that I had been working, but that wouldn't stop me. While God had my undivided attention, he started dealing with me on my writing. He gave me the vision and I sought it with my whole heart. I had rededicated my life and ended things with David.

I had made up my mind though that this time things were over. I just couldn't do it anymore. We stayed apart for a year. I was dedicated to the vision God had given me. I was writing and distributing my very own faith based newsletter in my hometown. I was selling advertisement spots in each issue to local businesses to cover the cost of printing. I didn't have any other job but my needs were being met financially and spiritually. I was so excited about what God was doing in my life and the response and support that I got was overwhelming. Temptation was lurking in the shadows. I ran into an old acquaintance, he actually had opened his own barbershop. I didn't think about our past that we shared, I was just thinking about him advertising in the newsletter. I vowed to keep it strictly business; I didn't think he was worth my salvation. It seems like I had made a deal with the devil.

I soon found myself in a compromising situation and once again, instead of asking God for forgiveness, I felt like a wretch that was so undeserving and now full of shame that I walked away from my ministry. Another skeleton got hung in the closet and this one would eat away at me. I even kept the truth from David. I don't know why he even felt the need to ask me about my personal life. "Hello, how are you?" I didn't even have to ask who was calling, I already knew. "Nothing much, are you coming to get the kids this weekend?" Strangely enough we were able to work out our own agreement for him to get the kids on the weekends and he was actually assisting me financially this time around. "Yes, I'm coming to get them." "Do you know what time?" "No, why are you asking so many questions? Must be some dude, who are you dealing with now?" I always took offense to his questions; he acted as if he knew me better than I knew myself. I knew the mistake I had made but it wasn't any of his business. "I hope you haven't had anybody around my kids. I guess what they say about your family is true." That's when I felt the blow from the knife. He killed me every time when he made those comments about my family and he knew it. Each time I would start crying, which made him think that I was lying even more. "No there is not a man in my life, let alone anyone coming around your kids." I hadn't lied, that was the truth. "Then why are you crying?" "I just hate when you automatically assume or make comments like I'm a tramp or something. You have no respect for me at all. You go out and do what you do and then you talk bad about me like I'm less of a person." "Well you better not have anyone around my kids and I'll be there to get them." He hardly ever said bye. I hadn't told him a lie but I couldn't tell him the whole truth. He kept his promise and picked up the kids.

I don't know how but the lie I told ended up bringing us together and I often wondered had I told the truth, if I would have been able to sever the soul ties for good. Just like all the other times before, I ended up pregnant again; no sooner than we got back together. This time it would almost cost me my life.

9 IS THERE LIFE AFTER DEATH

It was my last year in California, 3 days after my birthday and our third child was 5 months old. I had once again put David out, he had lost his job, was staying out all night, and instead of helping cut back on the bills by watching the children he refused. I was forced to pay a mortgage, childcare, a car note and all the other household bills by myself. I got him physically out of my house but the soul ties were so strong that he knew he could influence my thoughts and emotions. He would call and badger me about what I was doing, where I was going, whom I was talking to and accuse me of sleeping with any and everybody. I guess you can say I was at my breaking point. "David why did you come over here? I don't want you in my house. You don't just show up and demand me to let you see your kids. I hung up the phone on you for a reason. LEAVE ME ALONE! JUST GET OUT!" He always tried to intimidate me with his size. He would stand in front of the door so that I couldn't leave. He didn't care if the kids were around to witness everything. He would make it seem like I was the one that was crazy. "You stupid B*&!# you better get away from me. You are so stupid and crazy. Nobody wants your rundown self. I got a girl, now what? She better than your stupid A#&. She has way more than you do anyways. I need to get my stuff and I'm out. I don't want anything to do with you. I dare you to go to the courts too, I bet you don't get a penny. I ain't helping you with nothing." I don't know what made me snap. It wasn't like I hadn't heard all of this before but something hit a nerve. I remembered the prescription that was still in the cabinet and I poured as many pills as my hand could hold. I took each pill one by one. He continued to pack his stuff and call me stupid. He even started getting the kids things. He was going to leave me for dead. I crawled into my bed as I began to grow increasingly tired. I don't know how or even if it was me who called my mom, but my mom was on the other end of the phone. I am not even sure what was said, but soon after the phone call, my mother was at my home. I remember the sirens and vaguely being carried away, but shortly after everything went black. I didn't know if I was dead or alive. I remember once we got to the hospital, I was forced to drink some black liquid that forced me to throw up and then I went out again. What had I done? Where were my babies? Lord please don't let me die and go to hell.

It must have been hours later before I came to. I don't know if I had been in a deep sleep or unconscious. I opened my eyes and my mother was sitting next to my hospital bed. I didn't say much. I was still a little out of it. I asked my mother what had happened. "Rhachelle, you had me worried. I didn't know if you were dead or alive. All I could do was pray. What happened? You know when I got to the house, he was packing up his stuff. He was going to leave you to die." "I'm sorry mom. I just couldn't take it anymore. I'm tired." I began to cry. "Don't talk too much, just keep yourself calm." I lay there and just looked at her.

10 NEW STATE, SAME STATE OF MIND

Recovering was hard, I think I just acted as if nothing had ever happened. My immediate family kept everything a secret, so I had to just deal with everything internally. I made a doctor's appointment with my primary doctor to talk about things. She diagnosed me with anxiety and possibly post-partum depression. It all sounded good but I refused to take the medication. I mean I realized that I was not the same person before I started dating David, but I also knew that medication was not the answer. So I dealt with it the best way I could, I turned to recklessly smoking marijuana and drinking. And the rollercoaster with David started all over again.

The doctor took me off work for a while, I was in no condition to work but at the same time I was the only one supporting me and the children. The mortgage still had to be paid, along with all the other bills. I couldn't get myself out of the rut, I was tired. I reached out to Monique, but she was all the way in Vegas. "Hey Monique, how are you?" "Hey Chelle, pretty good, how are you and the kids?" We had barely started the conversation and I was already in tears. "Monique, I'm just tired. I feel like I just need to get away from here. I am tired of dealing with David and he just won't go away." I knew in my heart, that I didn't want to leave the rest of my family, but I was so used to running that I thought if I ran further away it would solve things. "Well Chelle, why don't you and the kids come out here, I'll help you with the kids. At least then you can get back on your feet." I knew Monique would help the best way she could, but no one knew that I was once again expecting another child; number four.

I started staying over my mother house more and going home less. David started staying back with his mother, so he really didn't know much about my plans. I mean he had heard a conversation or two but I think he had it in his mind that I would never leave. My mother was in support of me leaving, but I think she was just tired of dealing with the situation. Monique had always played the role of mother in my life anyways. I remember the day that I decided to relocate. It wasn't planned out by any means. I packed two suitcases with some of our stuff. I left my car at the mechanics and I purchased three Greyhound bus passes, the baby traveled as a lap child. It was the longest ride ever, I didn't have a going away party, no one really new. My mother made no big fuss, she dropped us off and we were on our way.

We were on the last bus of the evening; the kids slept most of the trip. I cried as we traveled from one city to the next. I was afraid. I didn't know what this sudden change would bring. Ultimately, I doubted that I would be able to stand on my own two feet. I never realized that I had been doing it along. I had been told so many times that I shouldn't, couldn't and wouldn't that I had actually started believing that I wasn't. The problem was is that I had lost all confidence in myself, so no matter how far I went my state of mind is what needed to change.

After 14 long hours, we made it to Las Vegas, NV. We weren't expecting the heat that met us, but we would adjust rather quickly to the desert summers. I immediately began searching for jobs and was fortunate to find one after just two weeks. I had spent so many years in banking that obtaining a job was easy. The only problem now was that I wasn't prepared to move into my own place, in a new city and with 3 little ones and one on the way. Out of fear, I called David and begged him to move, at least until I got situated. We even talked about starting over, how it might be better for us to be away from everything and everybody. I should have known something wasn't right when he didn't really object, but it wasn't like he had anything going for him and he would make sure to keep it that way.

11 WHAT DOESN'T KILL YOU WILL MAKE YOU STRONGER

Just like every time before, things didn't get better. I started working my job and of course David watched the kids, but he began to resent me. He blamed me that he couldn't go out and get a job, even though he never spent any time applying. But it just seemed like nothing that I ever did lasted anymore. The situation between us was bad, he continued to take, manipulate and when things didn't go his way he would hop on a plane and leave. Home life once again began to affect me on my job. I always tried to keep a smile on my face, but when I wasn't smiling I was complaining about how I felt things should be at work versus how they were. However, at the same time, I put a lot of effort into the work I was doing. I received a lot of praise for my hardwork, but I was still under a lot of pressure. Things just weren't right at home and one simple mistake at work, cost me my job. I was angry, but at the same time I was tired of banking. I had been applying for other jobs and I had finally heard back from a County job I had applied for but I knew I would have to play the waiting game on that one.

All stability had been lost when I started dating David, so I wasn't surprised when we got evicted soon after I was let go from the bank. He refused to work even during that time. I was working but only part time and not making close to what I had been making at the bank. It wasn't rocket science that I wouldn't be able to do it by myself, but he didn't care.

I couldn't take it any longer. I was tired of his routine. We had already lost our apartment, forced to live in a weekly one bedroom motel and as soon as I came in from work, all he could think about was leaving to go get high; that lifestyle hadn't followed me to Las Vegas. Little did he know, I had already planned my departure, I knew his routine so well, that all I had to do was come up with a plan. I was in contact with one of my old co-workers. She told me she would help me. I didn't have a car, more only means of transportation had been the bus. Packing up four kids on the bus with the personal possessions we had been able to keep before we had been put out was not possible, I set up the day and time with. We packed up everything, piece by piece into the car. The children didn't know what was going on, all that mattered to them was that we were together. A friend of mine that I had met at the little part time job I had gotten said that it would be okay if me and the kids came and stayed with her for a while until I got on my feet. She even watched the kids for me while I was work. It was a big adjustment for us all, I had never lived in the projects, matter of fact, I don't think I had ever been inside one until I moved all my belongings into the downstairs bathroom she had cleared out for me. In the middle of the room was two double size mattresses, with no bedframe, on the cold tile floor, up against a white-painted brick wall. This would be our refuge for several weeks.

    I would also have to adjust to a completely new routine. Prior to me moving in, the gas had been turned off. Luckily it was summer time, but I would learn all about drawing a bath. A neighbor had been kind to let her use their plug it stove. So we had two stove tops to use to cook and to use to boil water for bathtimes. I would bathe the children at night in a few inches of water, soap them up really good and get them ready for bed. In the morning, I would repeat the same routine for me. The sacrifice was hard but finally being away from the man that had dragged me so far down was undeniable. Some nights I slept with one eye open and the other shut, in order to prevent any of the other midnight crawlers from getting onto the bed. The building had a bad infestation of roaches; I seemed to fear them more than they feared me. The only hope I had left was the job interview that I had with the County before I moved.

So each day I continued in the routine from the previous day. I woke up before anyone else in the house, drew my bath water and waited at the bus stop to get to work. Some nights I cried myself to sleep, asking God why me, why am I going through all of this. I knew I hadn't been living the life that I knew to live but I just felt hopeless. When I would come home from work, I always made sure to bring the kids a treat, as if it would make them forget everything we were going through. My daughter may have been experiencing the hardest time adjusting and I just couldn't stand to have her living in such a way so one day I got the courage to call my sister and have her come and pick her up. She stayed for a few days and then came back. I think my sister saw the pain in my eyes. If I had stayed in longer in that environment, I would have become my circumstances. But I had a little bit more fight in me. I just wanted a little time away and my sister wanted me to watch her kids for her. So I agreed. One day turned into a week, a week into a few months, I stayed with my sister and her family. I continued to work my job, getting on the bus every morning, until the one day that I went into work and my supervisor called me into his office. He said my sales had been low so they were going to have to suspend me and he would let me know when I could come back. In other words, the economy was declining and timeshares were not selling like they use to.

I left work thinking what would I do now. No job, no place and I knew my sister's home wasn't a permanent option. The bus ride home was the longest that day. But it would be the last time that I would ride the bus for a while. When I made it back to my sister's house the mail had ran. I just so happened to have a letter from the County. I immediately ripped it open. There inside was my offer letter for employment. My hardwork was finally starting to pay off. I made sure to follow up with the Human Resources Department and confirm that I accepted the job. I wouldn't start my training academy for two months, but having a job offer with a decent pay was good enough for me.

12 FINDING MY WAY BACK

It took years of let downs and disappointments to realize that the love I had learned to give should have never been taught. Love cannot be bought, manipulated, it doesn't hurt, it doesn't lie, it doesn't abandon but instead it covers. I realized the type of love that I wanted and yearned for was the love I had been taught about in church. I had to find my way back to my first true and real love. I had to learn to stop separating my home life from my church life. I needed the same love that overshadowed me at church to overshadow me in my home, on my job and be demonstrated towards my children.

I was holding onto so much pain, bitterness, anger, unforgiveness and sorrow. I was being robbed of totally experiencing God's love and life. I had to start back from the basics and that was in prayer. I prayed and cried and prayed some more. Then I read my Bible, prayed some more and cried a whole lot more. God had started to take me through a process and all I knew I was feeling a lot better than I had before. David and I had finally went our separate ways. I was done but he wasn't convinced that it was over. I had taken him back so many times before. He would call a few times a week. "Hello," "What's going on?" That was his favorite line and no matter how many times I asked him to address me in a different way, he couldn't just say hello back. Did he really want to know what was going on? The house is a mess, your two youngest children have diapers that reek of this morning's oatmeal and apple juice and I'm still wondering how I'm going to pay the rent that was due last week. Of course he didn't want to hear that because he never concerned himself with it. "I miss you all. I really want my family back together." I never fell for that line. What he actually meant to say was I don't know how you did it all these years, working and paying bills, I'm tired of working and I need you to take care of me.

"Well missing us and wanting your family back together is one thing, but actually being a father and taking care of your responsibility is another. It also is not a reason for us to get back together." I finally was starting to stand my ground and making it clear to him that nothing he could say would ever bring us together. He then asked "Do you even still love me?" I know my response wasn't what he wanted to hear but it was sincere. "I will always care about you and pray that you reach your full potential." He immediately questioned my response, "That's not what I asked you if you were asking me then I would say yes or no but if you wanted 2 know my answer it is yes but answer mines." It was time for me just to say it like it was. "The kind of love that I have is that of a friend. I've realized that in order for me to love someone else I have to fall in love with myself again. You took that away from me and for that I could never open my heart up to you again." I felt so much better getting that off of my chest. His response was exactly what I expected because he, just like I, didn't know how to love. "Oh, ok." He never apologized; he never accepted responsibility. But I knew that I had to forgive him in order to move on and get the healing that I really needed most.

The kids were a whole different story. David had planted a seed in the oldest two that caused so much division and disregard. They didn't respect me as their mother, they talked back, they lied and they laughed right in my face. I thought I could just love the hell out of them, but it was going to take so much more. I had to also change. I spent so much time yelling and throwing fits that they no longer wanted to hear anything come out of my mouth. Then it hit me, "Shamar and Willie can you come in here please?" "Yes mom." I spoke in a very soft voice, if either one of them made a remark they wouldn't have been able to hear. "I know we have been through a lot and at times you may not want or think you don't have to listen me. I am your mother and from now on, I am not going to raise my voice or yell. It is killing me and it is not resolving anything. The both of you need to stop yelling as well. Is that understood?" They appeared to have been listening, "yes mom".

They had witnessed so much during my relationship with David. For some reason, David never thought it was important to shield them from anything. I did my best to shelter them from as much as possible. But David had always made it a point to belittle me in front of them, he always spoke against any other adult figure whom they should have listened to and he portrayed life as one big game. They had been there every time the police had to be called, when David got out of line and refused to leave the house. When he punched through doors, the first time he ever hit me, then ripped the phone out of the wall so I couldn't call for help and called me out of my name, they had seen it all. I couldn't move forward and act like it didn't happen, it would become our topics of discussion, our area of change and our demonstration of how we would not communicate to one another. We had to redefine love and learn of its attributes.

I didn't expect immediate change but I hoped to see a few changes, which I did. The change that I was making took a lot of effort but it seemed to be helping. You the soul ties had forced a lifestyle on me that I was not used to living but had very easily adapted. I know longer kept my house. I was never had much company because I was too embarrassed at all the mess. I didn't realize how much I needed to change until I was forced to look at all my issues face to face. I didn't know how to give or receive love. The love that I had learned I should have never been taught but the love of my father that had sustained me, but I didn't know how to show it.

Fortunately, Kimmy was still in my life and just a phone call away. After all the years of drama, I could no longer hide the issues that I had dealt with or were experiencing now. Kimmy never judged, she encouraged me and made sure to let me know that I could make. Kimmy had gone through some of her own dramas in life but she was always able to bounce back from them. The relationship with her and her mother had grown so strong and when life decided to take unexpected turns she was able to go to her and she trusted her advice because she had been there. I stopped giving Kimmy advice and gladly started taking it. She understood not only the situation but also the difficulty with walking away. I remember our conversation like it was yesterday. "Hey what's up?" Kimmy already knew who it was. Every time we talked it was like we had just seen each other, time and distance didn't matter, we had been through so much together. "Nothing much. I am feeling so much better. Taking control of my life and making necessary changes in my home. How are you feeling?" Kimmy had let me know she was expected a few weeks ago. Her life was changing for the positive, she had gotten married to a nice young man, she was attending church regularly, growing her business and enjoying life. "Yes! I knew you would. You are so strong. Don't let the devil and the spirits he put in other people take over. Fight him with your spirit sword. Lol! I'm hungry all the time. It's weird. Are you going to stay out there still?" Once Kimmy had finished college, we ended up living a lot closer to one another and with all my life dramas, I had ended up being the one to move away. "Yeah I don't know how much longer I'm going to stay here. I'm fighting with my entire being. I'm a survivor. I hope I can come out there soon." Even though I wasn't far, the cost always added up and I never had the extra money to visit as often. "Yep. I knew that when I met you. After all you were an honor student and president of an organization." I don't think Kimmy realized that all these years I had been looking up to her; she was the survivor. She had confronted all of her skeletons head on, I was just learning how to expose mine and let them go. "Thank you for being there through all this. I didn't realize how much being in the relationship with David and dealing with my mother all these years had damaged me. I'm getting back to that old Rhachelle and I'm loving it." It's a shame that not very many people had the opportunity to get to know the real me before David, but I was slowly but surely coming back.

"Yes, I've noticed." Kimmy replied. "Well I better let you go girl. I love you and take care of that baby." "Love you too Rhachelle and I will. Talk to you soon, bye." "Bye Kimmy."

That Sunday the kids and I attended church. We hadn't been in a while but the children always enjoyed. I like this particular church because it had children's church and you could feel the love from the moment you entered the door. I had made it on time to hear the Pastor bring the message. He was talking about "Letting Go to Let God". Every time I attended church the message was always just for me.

"Turn with me in your Bibles to Mark 3:27, and it reads, No man can enter into a strong man's house and spoil his goods except he will first bind the strong man; and then he will spoil his house. It got a little quiet in here. A lot of you are allowing people and things into your house, your mind, and your spirit and in your circle that shouldn't be there. We you are seeking the Lord you must seek him with your whole heart, stay in prayer and fast. The devil will look for any opportunity to get in your mix. When the spirit man is weak, other spirits will seek to bind us, they are like leeches they need a host. Just like in the garden of Gethsemane, while Jesus was praying to his father, the devil thought he could temp him and get in his house, make him change his mind, and abandon his purpose. We have to recognize when the enemy is attacking and call him out. Get thee behind me satan.

We'll let our friends talk us into going somewhere, hanging out and think its no harm. While deep down praying for a way out. We've allowed some of our very own friends to bind themselves to us. You give the excuse; we grew up together. Just because you grew up together does not mean you need to die and go to hell together. Saints we have to wake up and recognize when and how the enemy is trying to attack.

Some of you out there are holding onto garbage from your past. Those things mama always told you not to repeat outside the house. Tell mama I said, You walking around wondering why everytime you get in the church and decide to get your life together you end up back where you started or further away. You're holding onto bitterness, hurt and anger, then the enemy is binding lust, fornication, lying, and all types of spirits to your spiritual man. You're holding onto failed relationships, shattered dreams and empty promises. LET IT GO.

Forgiveness is a powerful weapon against the enemy. When we forgive we are releasing the power and control that the person who wronged us had. We are releasing the bind that seeks to prevent us from truly being in the will of God and experiencing that love. Forgiveness is that subtle issue in our hearts that allows those big issues to creep. Some turn to drugs to heal the hurt, alcohol, sex and even death. We need to forgive. Now that doesn't mean let Tom back into your life or start hanging with old friends. In some cases you may even have to leave your mother and father alone, but forgive them. Salvation is something to be desired, its a personal walk of faith and sometimes you will walk alone. But understand what my God said he would do, I'll never leave you or forsake you. I'll be a present help. He said he'd prepare a table in the presence of your enemies. Get out of the way and let God.

I'm closing, but I would like to ask if there is anyone that needs prayer?" I knew I needed to make my way to the altar. The message had spoke directly to me and I needed God to move on my behalf. I was halfway to the altar, eyes already swelled up with tears before I realized I had already gotten out of my seat. My hands were lifted up to the Lord in total surrender. I was tired of doing things on my own and my way. I needed guidance. I began to cry out to the Lord. "Forgive me Lord, I'm sorry. Restore me Lord, restore my faith, my peace and my joy. Lord I'm tired and I need you right now. Lord I thank you. Lord fix my heart, my mind and my soul. I'm yours Lord." I could feel the weights and the burdens being removed. I felt the change right there. The Pastor spoke to congregation one final time. "I want each one of you that are in the audience to find someone on the altar and tell them you love them. Sometimes we need to feel the power of God's love. When you except the Lord into your life, you accepted an entire family in the Body of Christ."

I hadn't enjoyed church so much in a long time. I knew in my heart that this was when life would change forever. I made up in my mind that I had to show God just how serious I was. Everything I did became a form of worship, when I cleaned, when I cooked, helped the kids with homework, gave them their bath and we even started praying together daily. I believed that if I showed God just how sincere my heart was, he would take care of the rest. I was starting to understand all of my issues and I was throwing out all the skeletons in my closet. See all the times before, I had been too embarrassed or shameful to let them all go, which had been preventing me from completely surrendering. But I was letting it all go this time around and was feeling lighter by the day.

13 AN OPEN LETTER OF FORGIVENESS

It took years, a lot more mistakes, a lot of reflection and praying before I came to the understanding that I was in control. I had to quit living life in my head, which was consumed with my past and start living in the now. I realized that I couldn't go back and fix things, I couldn't make my mother be a better mother and I couldn't make David be a better father. I had to start from the present and focus on the now; in that now was my life; a mother that was learning, healing and growing. Life couldn't be better.

The only problem was that even though I realized the issues were my mothers, she never realized she had any. I had to forgive her and also excuse her from my life. I had to learn to love her at a distance, so that her issues didn't become my own. I couldn't figure out the best way to communicate this to her, so one day I just started writing. I felt like I could put it all on paper and wouldn't be cut off, ridiculed or blamed. I just wanted her to know exactly how I felt, words from my heart.

Dear Mom,

Its been a while since I wrote you a letter. Do you remember when I was little and would write how I felt and leave it on your pillow? Well times haven't changed much. I always felt like if I just put it down on paper you would understand where I was coming from and would be able to reflect. So please as you read this letter, please dig a little deeper and look a little closer and hopefully you will see the world through my eyes.

Growing up, I always thought that some of the things I went through weren't normal, actually flat out dysfunctional. I can appreciate the fact that church was a must but I wish it had been actually applied. I never understood the name-calling, the putdowns, the constant ridicule or even all the physical altercations, it all seemed to conflict with the message of "God is Love". Every time I tried to bring things that bothered me to your attention, you acted as if it never happened. You offered no apologies and actually a lot of times you transferred the blame on me. I knew what I felt in my heart was right, but you led me to believe I had created or caused all the issues between us.

Your ridicule and put downs, created self esteem issues. Your lack of guidance and nurture lead me down a road of some terrible mistakes. I learned how not to submit within a relationship, how to substitute material possessions for love, how to blame instead of accepting fault and for a while I believed that I would never be anything. I started things and never finished them. I doubted and second-guessed myself on everything. I wanted to succeed but the failures made me feel that at times you were right.

Then one day I figured that the best answer that I could ever get would be found within those sixty-six books of the Bible. I read and I read, I reflected, I prayed and God revealed to me so many truths that I hadn't experienced. I realized why I had such a hard time surrendering. It wasn't that I didn't completely believe in God, but I didn't believe that I could actually reach a point of complete forgiveness. See "what goes on in this house stays in this house" wasn't just holding things back within my physical home but it was holding things back in my spiritual temple. I finally realized I could let it all go and be forgiven of it all. I could no longer hold on to the bitterness and anger, because it allowed so many other issues to attack my spirit. I'm not sure how you will feel about everything after reading this letter but I have drawn a conclusion. You will always be my mother, but you will no longer have any power to also be my source of pain.

I am reclaiming power over my life and the people I allow in it. You see those seeds that you planted in me, I also planted them in the hearts and minds of my own children. I am uprooting and killing that seed, for it will no longer have any power. I am raising my children the best way that I can, to fear God, be obedient and have faith. I am setting the example, and its not one that requires them to do as I say and not as I do. We pray together, we talk about everything and I make myself available to them to come to me with their problems. I'm choosing my words a lot better. I mean they are children and they are going to make mistakes, but I have to make them believe that they can and will do better. They will be great, they will succeed and they will reach their dreams as long as they focus and keep striving. I am their greatest advocate and supporter, not the biggest source of negativity and competition.

Mom my wish is that you put your life in God's hands and truly surrender. None of us can change the past, but we can change the now and look towards a brighter future. I forgive you. I love you. I'm closing this series in my life because it has definitely been longer than a chapter and there are no plans for a sequel. All things do happen for a reason and because of the life once lived, I discovered my purpose. I don't write this as your daughter, but I write it as Mother to Mother.

14 MY SEED WILL BE BLESSED

Everyday was a struggle, raising four boys and a girl on my own. I would pray, read my word and try to stay connected. I had to be honest with myself, accept my areas of weakness, learn how to develop those areas but most of all make some new habits. Some days were better than others but the devil had determined what my weakest point was and was putting me to the test. He was able to keep me blinded by love for years and bound by a relationship because I wanted a family for my children. Instead my family became the breeding ground for the continued dysfunction that I spent my early years in life avoiding. But God had given me another chance to be the best mother I could be. What the devil meant for evil, God was already working it out for my good. The devil planted seeds of doubt and put thoughts in my mind like, "you're in the house everyday, no job, no one even comes to see if you and the kids are okay, you are nothing and never will be, just give up now." But the God I serve would not allow me to rest. I would write, blog and meditate on God's love and purpose for my life. I realized that all things do work together for a reason. I spent more time with my children in those months than I had during all my working days. I began to instruct them according to the Word of God, obedience and faith in God is the necessary ingredients. I had to change the love that I had been so use to showing and actually start demonstrating it more affectively in my words and actions not materials. I also began to listen. My children began to tell me what they needed to change and even told me what I should do to see that change through. The yelling had to stop. A lot of times with the yelling came anger and frustration. We all were in need of learning a little more patience.

The more time I spent with them, the more they learned of my ways and the more time I spent with God, the more his ways were shown through me. Being a parent is a learned task and our first teachers are our own parents. I learned a lot from my mother but most of it should have never been taught. I also learned a lot from my father but didn't have the skills to apply it. See I adopted most of my behavior from the most dominant person in the home. I learned to yell, ridicule, show love through materials, and I focused on me. I didn't know how to encourage my own and push them to be better than me. I didn't realize how important my father's constant words of encouragement, patience, love, guidance and nurture had been. He was showing me God's love the entire time but my understanding was stifled because of everything else that dominated it in my home. I realized who the best teacher was and also found the best manual. I emptied my soul of all the anger, bitterness, frustration, unforgiveness, doubt and fear. I replaced all the junk with the love of God.

We are victorious. The devil will show up in the very area of your life that you struggle the most with. I shut him down in so many other areas in my life that he sought to attack me through my very own children who I gave life. The Bible became my source of direction and guidance. I prayed and believed that God would reveal to me his very plan for my life as well as my children. The spirit of doubt, fear and frustration will no longer control me. I will not give up. I will not be defeated. I will declare the works of the Lord. I will raise my young boys to be young men and fear the name of the Lord. They will believe in his word and power. I will raise my daughter to be a virtuous young lady and grow into a woman that will worship the Lord with her whole heart.

15 HERE AM I, SEND ME

For years, I have asked the Lord, why so much heartache and pain. Why couldn't I have just lived the normal life that people assumed I was living. Why did it have to be so hard. The answer I received wasn't the easiest to swallow and it came with a task greater than me. You see my mother had given me back to the Lord while I was yet in her womb. I was his to be used for his service. The devil had been on my tracks since I was a little girl, seeking to devour, destroy and discourage me. He knew that if I could endure the trials and tribulation that I would come out as pure gold. I had been prophesied to many times as a child and even in my adult life. Out of rebellion and fear, I continued to run away from my calling. I had made up my mind a long time ago that I didn't want to be a missionary like my mother, I didn't want the title and little old me could not fulfill the ministry. I was comfortable sitting in the pews, whether it be in the front or the back and no one really knowing my name. But whose plans supercede God's plans, certainly not yours and definitely not mine.

March 3, 2010 marks the date, that the Lord began to remove the walls I had built up. My offense, though minor, stripped me of using my college education to hide behind. That was an accomplishment that I had used for years to cover up all the shame of my past. He also began to deal with me in three different areas: strongholds, surrendering and transparency. I finally began to see just how deceitful the devil had been. There were issues in my heart that had kept me in bondage since I was a little girl. My heart was masked with unforgiveness and bitterness towards my mother. These issues had been stored away so long that I had almost forgot what it felt to be able to completely open my heart to anyone. Not to mention, carrying around these issues for so long also made it easier for other strongholds to bind themselves to my spirit. Lust came along for the ride, envy, jealousy, manipulation, fear, doubt and the list goes on. The Lord started the pruning process, trimming back the hedges that had started to take root and were strangling my soul. Extreme measures had to take place in order to get my attention. I still tried to put up a fight. I was down in the dumps, depressed, angry and confused. I turned to gambling and drinking and still found no peace. I gambled my car note money away, money for my utilities and I hit my lowest. But God had his hand on me through it all.

I would be fortunate to get a job in May. My final paycheck had covered me from March to May, I would have to figure out a way to pay June's rent. The new job came just in time and it was an answer to a prayer. I worked, I was able to pay my bills, but I was concerned about my car. My breaks were sounding awful. Not to mention, though I knew what God wanted me to do, I still continued to ignore him. 4th of July weekend would come, I had just got approved for this program and they would pay my July and August rent. I was driving home from work. I had dropped off all the other passengers. I had picked my children up from daycare and we were right outside the gate to my home. I attempted to slow down but my brakes had completely gone out. My reflexes kicked it and I immediately slammed on the brakes. I had no financial means to get my car repaired but I had to have it towed before the HOA did. It would sit at the auto shop for 3 months. I was experiencing my Jonah moment. The Lord had my undivided attention and the necessary provisions had been made so there was no need for me to leave from his presence.

Sometimes we must look back in order to get a glimpse of what God has brought us from. He has been right here with me through it all and for that I must be obedient and answer the call. I share my thoughts, my feelings, my trials and my tribulations as a demonstration of God's faithfulness and love. The Bible says, whom he loves he chasteth. He has and is preparing me for a great work and this is only the beginning. How do you conclude something that has given you life; strengthened an unknown passion and gift? Well I just won't end it because though the pages end, a new life that is everlasting in Christ Jesus, has just begun. My Sunday brings no more mourning, I have found joy and every day brings new mercies.

ABOUT THE AUTHOR

Rhachelle Johnson, received her Bachelor's degree from San Francisco State University in Psychology, with an emphasis in Clinical Psychology, in the Spring of 2000. Born and raised into a family that worked with developmentally disabled adults. Rhachelle always had a heart of compassion for those in need of advocacy and care. She has volunteered and worked with numerous organizations, tutored children in foster care, volunteered in elementary special education programs, volunteered with adult mental health clients and has a heart for the youth in her local church. Rhachelle soon became a little weary, becoming unsatisfied with the work of some of the organizations she worked with and for. In her heart she always felt that more could and should be done.

Rhachelle is not only a writer, but also a philanthropist. During the course of her writing Sunday Mourning, she was inspired to found an organization called Mother 2 Mother CDC, an organization providing preventative services to at risk mothers and families.

Rhachelle realized her purpose after working for the Department of Family Services. She vowed before colleagues, "I will carry this burden for every mother, in order to prevent them from suffering from being separated from their children." This organization is a fulfillment of that commitment.

Rhachelle bares a testimony of triumph and victory, overcoming obstacles that now allow her to relate to mothers that may want to throw in the towel. She is a mentor, motivational speaker, entrepreneur, author but most importantly a humble servant of God. "He has turned my mess into a message and my test into a testimony."

Rhachelle Nicol'

Sunday Mourning

www.ingramcontent.com/pod-product-compliance
Lightning Source LLC
Chambersburg PA
CBHW022305060426
42446CB00007BA/601